MASTERMIND

MASTERMIND

ALI FRIEDMAN

NEW DEGREE PRESS

COPYRIGHT © 2019 ALI FRIEDMAN

MASTERMIND

ISBN   978-1-64137-214-5   *Paperback*

          978-1-64137-215-2   *Ebook*

To both of my grandmas—Nana and G'ma—who taught me the meaning of true strength and perseverance

CONTENTS

When we deny our stories, they define us. When we own our stories, we get to write a brave new ending.

—BRENÉ BROWN

INTRODUCTION

———

*I'd never heard of any pro athlete talking about mental health, and I didn't want to be the only one. I didn't want to look **weak**.*

—KEVIN LOVE, CLEVELAND CAVALIERS

If you are a basketball fan, you've probably heard of Kevin Love: an NBA player for the Cleveland Cavaliers and a 6′10″ five-time All-Star. More recently, you might have even heard of him as a mental health advocate.

On November 5, 2017, Kevin Love's reality was shaken.

The Cavaliers were playing against the Hawks that day. Love felt that something was off. After halftime, he suffered a panic attack—his first.

All at once, the air around him felt heavy, his surroundings started spinning, and he couldn't quite seem to catch his breath. The assistant coach was yelling something about the next play, but Love was unable to make out what he was saying.

Love bolted to the locker room to get some air, in a desperate attempt to figure out what was happening to him.

"I was running from room to room, like I was looking for something I couldn't find," Love described. "Really I was just hoping my heart would stop racing. It was like my body was trying to say to me, *You're about to die.* I ended up on the floor in the training room, lying on my back, trying to get enough air to breathe."[1]

He was rushed to the hospital, where a battery of tests were run, but they did not detect anything unusual. Despite the confusion and trauma, Love was back on the court two days later for the next game.

Chances are you have heard the term "mental health" before.

---

1   Love, Kevin. 2018. "Everyone Is Going Through Something | By Kevin Love." *The Players' Tribune.* https://www.theplayerstribune.com/en-us/articles/kevin-love-everyone-is-going-through-something.

But what exactly falls under that umbrella, and what is so significant about it? If your middle school health class experience was anything like mine, your teacher might have briefly mentioned the concept before moving on to discussing the importance of a healthy diet and the harms of smoking.

While eating healthy and avoiding cigarettes are worthy topics to discuss, there is much more to learn about the mind and body.

The brain serves as the center of the human nervous system, and we undoubtedly could not function without it.

Mental health encompasses our emotional, psychological, and social well-being. It affects how we think, feel, and act. It also helps determine how we "handle stress, relate to others, and make choices."[2]

This definition may sound glaringly obvious and self-explanatory, but even today, there seems to be a lack of emphasis on mental well-being.

For someone like Kevin Love, there was no mental treatment or coaching for a panic attack. Doctors looked at his

---

2   U.S. Department of Health & Human Services. 2019. "What Is Mental Health?"MentalHealth.gov.

vitals, saw they were normal, and sent him back to play two days later.

Now imagine if, instead of a panic attack, Love had rolled an ankle. The Cavaliers have invested well over $100 million into this player, and they have teams of doctors, machines to diagnose any *physical* injury, rehabilitation systems, tools and technologies, and an approach to ensure Love is back on the court and not at risk of any long-term harm to his ankle.

There is a serious disconnect—one that affects not only athletes at the highest levels of sport, but all of us.

THE MENTAL HEALTH STIGMA

In 1999, the U.S. surgeon general labeled stigma as the biggest barrier to mental health care. Stigma tends to manifest itself as social distancing, in which people with mental issues are "isolated from others."[3]

As humans, we struggle to understand things we cannot see or diagnose or observe.

---

3   Friedman, Michael. 2014. "The Stigma Of Mental Illness Is Making Us Sicker." *Psychology Today.* https://www.psychologytoday.com/us/blog/brick-brick/201405/the-stigma-mental-illness-is-making-us-sicker.

The brain remains complicated and misunderstood. If something is "off" or "wrong," we tend to get uncomfortable and distance ourselves from it.

In fact, within most modern societies, attitudes that view symptoms of psychopathology as "threatening" and "uncomfortable" linger and contribute considerably to fostering discrimination toward those with mental health issues.[4] According to the World Health Organization, not only does mental illness affect people's well-being, but it also represents "the biggest economic burden of any health issue in the world."[5]

Of the reported 450 million people across the globe who suffer from mental health conditions, 60% of them do not receive any care whatsoever. 90% of those in developing countries receive no care.

Why are we so quick to shy away from mental health?

After his on-court panic attack, Kevin Love was predominantly concerned that others would find out about his incident. Love never imagined that he, of all people, would be

---

4   Davey, Graham. 2013. "Mental Health & Stigma". *Psychology Today.*
     https://www.psychologytoday.com/us/blog/why-we-worry/201308/
     mental-health-stigma.

5   Friedman, *Psychology Today.*

susceptible to panic attacks, or that the sphere of mental health was anything he would ever have to think about.

It was certainly a wake-up call. Why was he so concerned that other people would find out about his panic attack? Would they view him differently? Treat him differently? Look down on him?

As a professional athlete, physical well-being is obviously a huge part of the game. But what about mental health—where does that come into play? Can athletes truly be physically healthy and performing at the highest levels without taking their mentality into account?

These are all questions that enveloped Love after that consequential game on November 5.

He didn't want his teammates to view him as unreliable, and up until that point, he had always considered mental health to be someone else's problem. But after his own episode, which seemed to come out of nowhere, Love realized that mental health issues are as real as physical injuries, like a broken leg or a dislocated shoulder.

The Cavs helped Love find a therapist. While he had his doubts and reservations, he was open-minded enough to make an appointment.

"I'm the last person who'd have thought I'd be seeing a therapist. I remember when I was two or three years into the league, a friend asked me why NBA players didn't see therapists," Love recalled. "I scoffed at the idea. *No way any of us is gonna talk to someone.*"[6]

Unfortunately, mental health remains a taboo topic, and people often associate mental illness with weakness (whether consciously or subconsciously).

Up until his first panic attack, Kevin Love had not given much thought to his mental health, but it quickly became a reality he was forced to deal with. While his experience with therapy has at times been awkward and trying, it ultimately has helped him begin to work through the challenges that have come his way.

Love emphasizes that he by no means has everything figured out, but he is working through it. At the end of the day, it is important to recognize that everyone is going through *something*. And whether or not that something is physically apparent to the naked eye, it's real.

As Love succinctly put it, **"Everyone is going through something that we can't see."**

---

6   Love, *The Players' Tribune.*

This book aims to squarely embrace that fact.

Those who accept the importance of mental wellness have an advantage over the rest of us.

I believe that mental wellness is the *Moneyball* of wellness — an advantage that isn't commonly understood yet and therefore benefits those who do understand it. In Michael Lewis' book, *Moneyball*, he famously details how Oakland Athletics used advanced analytics to gain an advantage over teams with larger budgets. This approach allowed them to not only be competitive but also vastly outperform their own expectations, despite their small budget.

I liken it to the advent of systematic athletic training in the offseason. If talent gets you to the upper echelons of anything, then you are competing against the best of the best. So finding advantages like offseason training or new recovery methods can be a way to gain our own edge.

We have seen how physical exercise can help us keep fit and healthy and enhance longevity. By the same token, mental exercise is also critical.

My hope is that by sharing the stories of how some of the world's most successful people in business, entertainment, sports, science, and technology use mental wellness to succeed, each of us can find our own strategies to harness the power of mental wellness.

To be clear, this is not a self-help book, or a thesis, or merely a compilation of research, but rather a discussion with others who have found methods that work for them, which may help you as a reader find your own path to wellness.

Although psychology was one of my majors, I have given my friends life advice (that they are bound to ignore), and I occasionally fantasize about becoming the next Dr. Phil, I am not an expert by any stretch of the imagination. And I certainly don't claim to have all the answers. In fact, my biggest motivation is curiosity.

This book is designed to capture insights from others and combine them into an approach that readers can glean their own strategies from. I made the difficult decision to share my own journey, with the aspiration that others might benefit and realize they are not alone. I am just a person with some valuable experiences who wants to shed light on the complex topic of mental health and encourage destigmatizing mental illness.

As I will expand on later, I have striven for perfection my entire life. I consider myself extremely fortunate in numerous ways: I have grown up with a supportive family, as well as an amazing group of friends and teammates, and I have been blessed with great educational opportunities.

Why would I ever be susceptible to any sort of mental illness?

What problems could I possibly have?

What do I have to complain about?

While I have always been sensitive to the issue and to those around me struggling with mental illness, I have to admit, like many others, I never thought for a second that I too might deal with something similar.

Mental illness affects more of us than we might initially think. Everyone knows someone going through something, whether or not it is considered a full-blown disorder.

I have more than a few friends who have grappled with eating disorders, depression, anxiety, and OCD, to name a few. And it effectively took years before they too felt comfortable enough to share their battles.

As I set out to write this book, I was absolutely terrified that revealing personal stories about my own struggles would make people see me differently—my friends, my family, employers. But after much thought, worrying, and deliberation, I recognized that this was precisely part of the problem.

I realized that (somewhat counterintuitively), true strength comes with vulnerability and the ability to open up about what you are going through. Expressing yourself. Admitting your flaws or failures and then learning from them to become even better.

My goal is that this book offers some value for every single person who picks it up, rather than strictly targeting those with mental illnesses or any niche group. Everyone has stress in their life and likely knows someone who suffers from a mental illness, so I hope this book will provide inspiration for how to better manage, or at least be aware of, your mental health in order to promote your well-being.

This book also highlights the more informal mechanisms that can be useful to nurture your health outside of more traditional therapy, emphasizing that both formal and informal strategies can greatly benefit anyone.

It's *doable.*

CHAPTER 1

OVERCOMING
THE STIGMA

———

Generally speaking, the attitude towards mental health issues is getting a renewed focus. But we in the past 30 years or so have lost so much ground that it's going to take us quite a while to catch back up.

—DEREK GAUNT, HOSTAGE NEGOTIATOR

According to the National Alliance on Mental Illness, approximately one in five adults in the United States experiences mental illness in a given year—that's 43.8 million people, an astounding 18.5% of the population. But adults aren't the only ones who suffer from mental illness: roughly 20% of youths between the ages of 13 and 18 experience a severe mental health condition as well.[7]

Derek Gaunt, a hostage negotiator, was assigned to investigate the murder of a little boy, who was eight years old at the time of his death.

The boy was playing with his sister in their grandmother's driveway when the perpetrator approached him. He never laid hands on the boy's sister, but he grabbed the little boy and nearly decapitated him with a knife.

Based on witness descriptions of the event and the reported behavior that the killer exhibited, Derek and his team knew they were dealing with and looking for someone with serious mental health issues.

"We put out a flyer with the best description we could come up with, and when you put out a flyer in the middle of a murder investigation, you're going to get inundated with leads," Derek explained to me. "Everybody's going to see it on the news, everybody's going to pick up the phone, everybody's calling in. It's really tough for us in law enforcement to put

---

7   "Mental Health By The Numbers | NAMI: National Alliance On Mental Illness." 2018. *Nami.Org.* https://www.nami.org/Learn-More/ Mental-Health-By-the-Numbers.

out information like that so early on in an investigation because you have to run down every one of them."

As part of the process, Derek was assigned to go out and track down some of the lead suspects, in an attempt to find the perpetrator of the heinous murder.

"I was floored by the number of verified schizophrenics, paranoid schizophrenics, that were walking around on the streets untreated. And many of these people were high functioning," Derek observed, reflecting back on this particular investigation that has stuck with him to this day.

A number of these identified high-functioning people with schizophrenia were actually able to maintain a job and were capable of holding a conversation. That being said, Derek noted that there still always appeared to be something missing with them.

"I didn't know the extent of the problem until this murder happened, and I went out and I started interviewing some of these people, and I was like, 'You gotta be kidding me,'" Derek recalled.

While there were a decent number of relatively high-functioning people with schizophrenia out in the community, there were many others further along on the spectrum.

"They were clearly, clearly out there. . . . They were on an island by themselves, and they were functioning under all kinds of hallucinations, and they were walking amongst the street. You see them all the time," Derek pointed out.

Back in the early 2000s, Derek noted a palpable disconnect between the reality of mental health issues and commonly held perceptions of them, but he had not realized the extent to which people affected by these conditions lacked adequate resources and support. While degrees of severity range when it comes to schizophrenia and mental illness in general, Derek observed that there seemed to be both a lack of understanding and a scarcity of resources to treat those affected.

We tend to think that mental illness is isolated to small segments of the population, but the truth is that the numbers of diagnosed *and* undiagnosed people suffering through mental illness are staggering.

A SNAPSHOT OF HISTORY

People with mental health issues have historically been treated differently, excluded from society, and even brutalized. This treatment may arise from the misguided views that people with mental health problems may be more violent or unpredictable than people without them, or are somehow just "different." There is no evidence, however, that these negative beliefs are grounded in fact.[8]

Early beliefs turned to demonic or spirit possession as the cause of mental health problems. The early medical model is a source of stigmatized views because it oversimplifies the causes of mental health issues to medical or physical dysfunction.[9] However, current research demonstrates that mental illnesses are inevitably shaped by cultural and environmental factors as well. For example, resignation syndrome is an illness solely reported among children of asylum-seekers in Sweden. Affected children withdraw completely, cease to walk or talk, or even open their eyes and don't react to physical triggers, such as a pinch or someone putting ice on their stomach.[10]

Additionally, the early medical model negatively characterized patients. This notion that "*mad* people cannot function properly in society, or can sometimes be violent," perpetuates the view that people with mental health problems are different and should consequently be treated with caution.[11]

8   Swanson, JW. 2015. "Mental Illness And Reduction Of Gun Violence And Suicide: Bringing Epidemiologic Research To Policy." *Pubmed Central*. doi:10.1016/j.annepidem.2014.03.004.

9   Davey, *Psychology Today*.

10   Pressly, Linda. 2017. "Sweden's Mystery Illness." *BBC News*. https://www.bbc.com/news/magazine-41748485.

11   Davey, *Psychology Today*.

* * *

"Just do it"—Nike's infamously coined slogan that has gained worldwide attention and recognition.

Have you ever gotten so used to a routine that it almost becomes mechanical? Like riding a bike, tying your shoes, or driving a car?

Something you are used to, something so ingrained in your system it requires almost no thought whatsoever? But then, in the event that you do happen to consciously think about what you are doing, just for a moment, you almost forget how to do it entirely? Like if you stop to think about the task at hand, one you have completed effortlessly millions of times before, all of a sudden it feels unnatural?

For a split second, I forgot how to drive.

Not in the sense that I forgot what a steering wheel was or which pedal was the brake. But nonetheless, in the blink of an eye, I started overthinking the process that had become so natural and second nature to me several years prior.

I hopped into the beat-up family minivan and started the engine. Without consciously thinking about it, I'm sure I moved my seat forward (short people problems) and adjusted my mirrors, before glancing behind me as I started cautiously backing the car out of the driveway.

I was heading straight down Wisconsin Avenue from my house to Georgetown, a route that I had taken countless times before. It was evening, but not terribly dark outside yet.

I turned on the radio, as I always do when I'm driving, and started getting lost in the upbeat pop music playing on 99.5—one of those songs that's catchy but basically played to death by the radio stations to the point where eventually you can no longer listen to a song you once enjoyed.

As I approached the halfway point to my destination, I started to panic. All of a sudden, I was hyper-aware of how fast the cars around me were zooming by. I noted each and every vehicle that was (impressively) parallel parked on either side of the narrow street, all of them packed together like sardines. Parallel parking was a task I'd avoided like the plague since passing my driver's test; there's just no room for error.

For some unknown reason, my mind was racing.

At any moment, someone in one of the parked cars could abruptly open their driver seat door, and it could slam into my beloved minivan. Even while driving cautiously, I really had no guarantee that every other driver—whether in a moving vehicle or a parked car—would be equally alert.

It only takes a *split second* to make a fatal mistake.

What if someone who isn't in my line of vision jumps out from behind a parked car? What if I hit someone? Could I live with myself? How do you come back from something like that?

A couple of impatient drivers aggressively laid on their horns, clearly oblivious to my panicked state.

Anxious thoughts, which had started abruptly and quite randomly, began to inundate my brain. The harder I tried to concentrate on something else, anything else, the more anxious I got.

I started spiraling.

I noticed how close in proximity the cars going in the opposite direction were to me and my minivan. While they were no doubt going at most five miles above the speed limit, they appeared to be racing, whizzing by just inches away from my car. I was almost certain a driver would ram into me at any moment. It was simply a matter of time.

It only takes one second.

In the blink of an eye, my life could end. One jerky movement, or one distraction, or one instant when there was a brief lag in someone's reaction time. That's all it takes.

Just do it.

The palms of my hands felt clammy, and I was sweating profusely. A couple teardrops fell onto the steering wheel, catching my attention and temporarily shaking me out of my trance. Without even realizing it, I had been quietly sobbing while driving.

There was literally nothing noteworthy about this night in particular. I was driving a route so familiar to me it required almost no effort to complete. There were no jarring accidents along the way, no hazardous weather conditions, nothing.

Just do it.

Yet somehow I managed to get so in my head about something that had never concerned me or even really crossed my mind before.

It only takes one second to make a fatal mistake. To change everything.

I had never been a paranoid or anxious person, but I couldn't seem to shake the weight of this heavy thought.

Just do it.

I think the lack of control was what hit me the hardest. In that moment, something so trivial and insignificant as driving ten miles completely shook my confidence.

If I couldn't control my own actions, what did I have? What was I really in control of in my own life? Certainly not my inner thoughts or anxieties.

In that instant, I realized that there are times when I couldn't just *do it.*

And I had to find a way to live with that thought.

NO ESCAPE IN SIGHT: STIGMA AND SOCIAL MEDIA

You're fat.

You're ugly.

You're dumb.

You're doing a man's job.

Why don't you just kill yourself?

You must be off your meds. You're nuts.

With the ever-growing prevalence of social media, attacks such as these have become almost commonplace.

Everyone has an opinion to voice. It's no secret that being in the public eye comes with its fair share of challenges and criticisms. Trenni Kusnierek, NBC Sports anchor and reporter, knows this well.

A few days before we spoke, someone told Trenni that she must be off her meds and needed to see a therapist.

"If I had cancer you would never say that to me," Trenni pointed out. "If I had heart disease and was open about it, you would never say that to me. So you don't get to say that about my mental health."

While it definitely helps to have thick skin in the TV and broadcasting industry, that alone only gets you so far.

Over time, Trenni has really come to value the importance of tailoring her social media accounts as much as possible, to avoid exposure to negative comments aimed directly at her.

"In order to keep my sanity, I pared down how much I use social media," Trenni explained to me. "I only see mentions from people that I follow. And if I don't like what you say, I don't like how you're speaking to me, I block you."

Although it is unfortunate that there are a number of people out there who post hateful comments from the shelter of their screens, in an increasingly connected and digital world, abstaining from social media isn't necessarily the best course of action. No one should have to give up Twitter because of the lack of sensitivity of their fellow tweeters. Trenni has personally found that the blocking function on Twitter provides her with a sense of relief and control over her account.

"There's not any question to ask," Trenni told me. "Like, we're not friends. We're not in a relationship. Twitter isn't a right. It's not a God-given right that you get to follow people and say whatever you want to."

"I don't owe you anything."

For one reason or another, offensive and hurtful comments frequently tend to surface on Twitter specifically, so Trenni is very cautious about posting pictures of her niece and nephew.

"I do it on Instagram a little bit," she said. "But I definitely will not do it on Twitter now, and I won't mention my family in a tweet or anything."

Not only do these negative comments affect her personally, but they also hurt her parents' feelings and cause them to worry about Trenni when they see such vitriol about her on social media.

"There's a trickle-down effect that people don't think about," Trenni explained.

Trenni has a friend who plays baseball who had posted a humorous tweet a couple of weeks earlier; Trenni quote-tweeted it with a funny comment. She soon went back and deleted her repost, however, due to concern that people would take it the wrong way. She was worried that fellow Twitter users were bound to speculate about their relationship or say nasty things about them.

"I was like, 'I just don't want to deal with it.' Like, 'I don't want him to have to go through it, and I don't want to have to go through it because it just makes you feel bad.' That's the other thing: it's not only you personally—you see how people treat your friends or your colleagues, and then you think about that too."

In an ideal world, everyone would keep their negative comments to themselves and not feel the need to post them publicly on social media despite the apparent lack of repercussions due to technology's distancing effect. But sometimes the best someone can do is find a way to limit their social media accounts in a way that works for them and reduces the amount of stress in their lives as much as possible.

It's all about finding little ways to take care of yourself. For Trenni, that fundamentally comes down to sleep, exercise, eating well, and meditation, all of which help her mentally prepare as best she can, so that when a stressful situation arises, she will be better equipped to handle it. In addition to focusing on these pillars, monitoring her Twitter usage and blocking unpleasant users when necessary also helps maintain her mental health.

"You can choose to not log onto Instagram or Twitter, but you can't always escape, especially if you're in the public eye. In some ways, there's no escaping it," Trenni mused.

It is important to be mindful of how your social media usage affects your mood and daily life. But instead of cutting it out entirely, it can be helpful to find seemingly small ways to adapt your experiences with social media, to promote your well-being and an overall healthier lifestyle.

* * *

Annika Cowles, a recent graduate of the University of the Arts, also has firsthand experience with the effects of harsh comments. Although not a sports anchor like Trenni, she is an actress and thus must also face the challenges and criticisms that come with being in the public eye.

"You're either skinny, or you're fat."

"And if you're fat, you're not going to work."

This assertion is the harsh reality of acting, which Annika finds problematic given that the average woman is a size 12. It's no secret that the life of a professional actor comes with a significant load of stress and self-doubt along the way. Being judged by others is essentially part of the job description.

"At the end of the day, it's us that we're selling," Annika explained to me.

The Friday we spoke in late October, Annika had just come from a meeting with a well-known LA manager, who was imparting some words of wisdom and advice on what kinds of characters she and her friend Jackson had the potential to play.

The manager turned to Jackson and matter-of-factly announced, "You need to lose twenty pounds."

Just like that. No sugarcoating whatsoever.

Every actor Annika knows devotes a significant amount of time and effort to maintain a healthy diet and a physically active lifestyle. Eating balanced meals, going to the gym, working out regularly—all the good stuff that we were advised to do in health class back in the day, but that seems impossible to fully achieve. There are only so many hours in a day.

Annika is a size four and weighs 125 pounds, but the manager even advised her to lose some weight.

"It would be great if you could get down to 120 pounds," he remarked.

After all, for actors, looks matter. And as the saying goes, the camera adds ten pounds.

Actors are under immense pressure and scrutiny, being in the public eye. A lot goes into promoting a healthy lifestyle; for actors, regular therapy is often a big component of that.

According to Annika, almost all of her friends go to therapy in addition to physical therapy. It's just what they do: a routine, in a sense. Part of the process.

On top of being a full-time college student and working two part-time jobs, Annika is constantly going out and auditioning for new roles. She has to memorize about five different scenes per week and find time to rehearse the plays with people who likely do not have the same schedule as she does, so she has to fit that into her plans. Not having a consistent schedule is tough, and it's certainly challenging to juggle auditions with school and just having a normal social life as well.

While Annika has been acting for years now and has grown accustomed to the demanding field and pressure of maintaining a certain image, the LA manager's blunt advice about her weight still affects her—even if in a more subtle way.

"It's something that's always going to be on the back of my mind," she admitted.

While Annika takes issue with people saying art *is* therapy, she does think art *can* be therapeutic, as it is a great outlet to express emotions. When you walk into the room for acting, you're expected to leave all your baggage behind. Luckily, Annika has found therapy to be a space that helps her do just that. Sometimes the chaotic lifestyle inherent to the acting world takes its toll and manifests itself in less healthy ways.

"Most actors I know smoke weed and drink like crazy," Annika observed. "I think it's something that we see in movies and television, and so that's how we think you deal with things."

When Annika was studying in London, her teachers would actually hand her the lines she had to memorize and tell her to go get a pint of beer at a bar to do so. It's certainly not uncommon for actors to go pound a few drinks before heading to an audition if they're feeling nervous—just to help take the edge off.

While having a couple of drinks every now and then isn't in and of itself cause for concern, the way in which these actors feel the need to consume drugs and alcohol to relieve their anxieties is emblematic of how being in a stressful environment can negatively affect your mental health.

Although the acting world comes with its fair share of stressors, Annika has found ways to preserve her mental health.

"I do a lot of stand-up comedy and try to deal with things by laughing about them," she explained.

Annika also likes to knit and read, and she tries to keep things out in the open rather than bottling her thoughts and emotions up.

Sometimes focusing on the little things that bring you joy—to defuse stressful situations and alleviate worrisome thoughts—truly goes a long way.

* * *

As demonstrated by Annika and her friends' use of therapeutic services, there is evidence that demand for mental health resources has increased over the past couple years. Yet the increase in demand has "sparked a fear, especially among college administrators, that young students across the country are becoming more sensitive and less resilient, which has fed a vigorous national debate between students, faculty, and universities about the treatment of mental health in classrooms," according to *The Atlantic*.[12]

12 Kwai, Isabella. 2016. "Today's College Students Are Not Less Resilient." *The Atlantic*. https://www.theatlantic.com/education/

Some universities, such as Oberlin, have proposed the adoption of trigger warnings: disclaimers meant to protect those who have experienced trauma such as sexual assault or violence, by "forewarning the appearance of disturbing material in text," the *Atlantic* article explains.[13]

An example of a trigger warning is provided by Oberlin's resource guide:

> We are reading this work in spite of the author's racist frameworks because his work was foundational to establishing the field of anthropology, and because I think together we can challenge, deconstruct, and learn from his mistakes.[14]

Although the implementation of trigger warnings is applauded by some students, others have responded with vehement pushback, according to *The Atlantic*:

---

archive/2016/10/the-most-popular-office-on-campus/504701/.

13   Ibid.

14   "Oberlin College | Office Of Equity Concerns | Support Resources For Faculty." 2019. *Oberlin Office Of Equity Concerns*. http://web.archive.org/web/20131222174936/http:/new.oberlin.edu/office/equity-concerns/sexual-offense-resource-guide/prevention-support-education/support-resources-for-faculty.dot.

Faculty questioned the loss of academic freedom, the *Los Angeles Times* called it "the glorification of victimhood," and Greg Lukianoff and Jonathan Haidt, in a widely dissected piece for *The Atlantic*, argued that such policies were enabling students to develop "extra-thin skins" by preventing them from feeling uncomfortable, objectively analyzing their emotional states, and overcoming their setbacks. The emerging picture of the hypersensitive, fragile college student is predicated, in part, on this statistical increase in demand for counseling services.[15]

---

15   Kwai, *The Atlantic*.

CHAPTER 2

AS REAL AS PHYSICAL PAIN

―

"Now she has a real reason to kill herself…"

"If you follow through with your thoughts of suicide, make sure you are successful."

"I don't feel bad for her; it was her choice."

"It would have been way better if she had died that day. She's a monstrous cripple now."

Her brother heard the ringing of the gun shot. He rushed to the bathroom and kicked the door in to find his sister, Katie, covered in blood.

Her face had been almost entirely blown off.

While eighteen-year-old Katie miraculously survived her attempted suicide, the effects were devastating, to say the least: she lost her mouth, nose, part of her forehead, and much of the bones that constitute the jaws. When she was wheeled into the Cleveland Clinic, her brain was essentially exposed. Her face would never be the same. Nothing else would; this was a matter of life or death.

Katie was given a second chance at life. She became the youngest person in the United States to receive a face transplant, one of just forty transplants of that nature ever performed in the world—she became the guinea pig in a still-experimental surgery.[16]

As you can imagine, reconstructing a face is an incredibly daunting and intricate task. Katie's powerful, heartbreaking story garnered a mixed public reception. While many applauded Katie, her family, and the countless doctors and surgeons involved throughout the process, there were many others who criticized Katie for "putting this" on her family. Some called her selfish; others exclaimed that they simply

---

16 Connors, Joanna. 2018. "How A Transplanted Face Trans-
    formed Katie Stubblefield's Life". *Nationalgeographic.Com*.
    https://www.nationalgeographic.com/magazine/2018/09/
    face-transplant-katie-stubblefield-story-identity-surgery-science/.

didn't feel bad for her, and it would have been better if she had succeeded in taking her own life:

"They should have let her go . . . this is too unfair."

"They are just punishing her for what she's done. How cruel and sadistic of their family."

"She is lucky. She chose to shoot herself in the face. They should extend help to people who were injured through no fault of their own first."

"Her parents should have allowed her to die that day. What they've done to her is unforgivable."

"The amount of money and time that has gone into this could be better spent elsewhere—those doctors and nurses could be helping someone who has fallen seriously ill, which wasn't self-induced. I think the whole thing is quite selfish."

"I'm surprised she didn't try to kill herself again."

"What made her do such a horrendous thing to herself???"

"She single-handedly ruined her and her family's lives."

The hateful, insensitive comments go on and on. The negative reactions to Katie's story clearly illustrate the stigma surrounding mental illness, such as depression and suicidal behavior, and point to the ever-pressing need to debunk the harmful misconceptions involved.

It is true that Katie's action in that fateful moment irreversibly changed the course of not only her own life, but also the lives of her family members. A second rarely passes when Katie is left unattended by either one of her parents. Together, as a family, the Stubblefields have undergone countless surgeries, doctor appointments, consultations, various forms of therapy—and the list continues. However, is it fair to assess her suicide attempt as "selfish," and should she shoulder all the blame for the consequences of her actions?

Based on the numerous judgmental remarks, it appears that people are missing the main point about Katie's condition: suicidal thoughts are *not* logical, and attempting to take your own life is by no means a rational act. Often, those experiencing suicidal ideation are not thinking clearly; when it gets to that point, they perceive themselves as a burden and believe they will be doing everyone else a favor by taking their own lives. While I recognize that mental illness can be difficult, if not impossible, to fully grasp if you do not struggle with it yourself, I could not seem to shake the glaringly damaging consequences of the misconceptions surrounding Katie's story.

* * *

I could literally hear my pulse throbbing. Even though my dorm room was silent, the pounding inside me was deafening.

I glanced at the time in the upper-right corner of my laptop screen. 4:38 p.m. I had a solid five minutes to compose myself before leaving for class. I couldn't be late to my own presentation.

It was a Thursday, my busiest day of the week in terms of classes. I absolutely dreaded going to my government seminar on Thursday nights. While I found the overall topic of religion and ethics in foreign affairs interesting, I was disheartened by the evident gap in knowledge between me and the rest of my classmates. It seemed like everyone else in the class somehow came in knowing every single detail there is to know about Catholicism and the history of religion.

Was I really the only one who didn't have a personal story about an encounter with the pope? What were these obscure countries that students were casually name-dropping in their examples, countries I had never even heard of, let alone knew anything about??

Before class each Thursday, I would inundate my textbooks with colorful sticky notes, marking what I thought were the "important" passages (although by the time I exhausted an entire pack of sticky notes for one of the three required course readings for that week's session, I realized it was challenging to find a passage that wasn't relevant).

I would stay up until the wee hours of the night (4 a.m. became the new 1 a.m.) crafting my response papers every week; no matter how far in advance I started doing the readings, I inevitably wouldn't be able to submit a complete response until the night before at the earliest.

I was set to give a presentation on the World Jewish Congress that particular Thursday. I had done the research and put together the PowerPoint slides. All I needed to do was stand up in front of the class and present them. This task wasn't something I had ever struggled with in the past—typical nerves before a presentation, sure, but nothing like this.

I was intimidated by my professor and classmates, and the thought of all those eyes on me during that presentation was crippling. Paralyzing.

I was so anxious about everything that could potentially go wrong that I was physically unable to practice my presentation beforehand, despite my best efforts. When the time came to present, it was consequently and unsurprisingly a train wreck. During the Q&A section, my classmates asked a few simple questions that I should have been able to answer. But my fear paralyzed me. I was unable to respond to how the congress is funded or basic questions about its founding. Under normal circumstances, I would be over-prepared for any presentation I had to give. The following day, I received an email from my professor with his feedback on my presentation:

"Ali, your topic was a good one, and your slides with their graphics were attractive. But your presentation was basic and your oral presentation added little to the information on the slides. Keeping the powerpoint slides spare as you did is right, but they shouldn't substitute for your presentation and control of the material..."

I was too humiliated to even read the rest of the email. I had been drained of all motivation and strength—both physical and mental. I truly felt like I was running on empty, with nothing left to give. Before the next class, I emailed my professor saying I had the flu. I couldn't bear to go after my flunk of a presentation, but I also couldn't bring myself to tell him the real reason why I couldn't get myself to attend. I briefly debated explaining my current mental health struggles but ultimately decided against it. A physical illness, like the flu, just seemed so much more tangible and legitimate than the mental illness I was grappling with.

In reality, this mental struggle was more debilitating than the flu. I'd been sick a number of times throughout my college years (Strep throat? Mono? Flu? Common cold? You name it; my poor immune system was not prepared for the college lifestyle). But this was a different beast altogether—the kind that prevented me from getting out of bed some mornings, where it took every bone in my body and every ounce of my effort just to get myself to shower and make breakfast.

I did not have the courage or strength to admit to my professor that I legitimately could not drag myself out of bed that morning. What would he think of me? I was terrified of coming across as lazy or unmotivated or as a student who didn't care about learning or doing well academically (this had never been the case for me). He was bound to think of me differently. After all, I had made it to my junior year in college and was on the dean's list every semester. How could I explain this? I couldn't understand it myself.

VULNERABILITY

This was it. The moment I had been anticipating for years now.

My fingers trembled slightly with excitement as I started typing.

I couldn't help but fantasize about how things could be: would our sleep schedules line up, would we live well together, sharing all of our deepest darkest secrets? Or could I be making an enormous mistake?

It had all been building up to this pivotal turning point in our relationship. We had shared everything—from our common running pastime (despite our love-hate relationship with the grueling sport), to our fond memories of our hometowns, to our mutual love and obsession with every single product artfully displayed in the aisles of Trader Joe's. What was left to discuss?

I took a deep breath and exhaled slowly. This was it. Time to pop the question.

Will you . . . be my . . . roommate?

As soon as I hit the enter button, I hastily shut my laptop and tried to distract myself to stop my mind from racing.

Vulnerability.

Although finding a college roommate freshman year might seem like a minor example of vulnerability, the concept itself holds true: I had put myself out there, laying everything on the line. And whatever happened next was out of my control.

In case you were wondering, it ended up working out perfectly; Lily and I hit it off and are the best of friends. We've spent multiple years sharing a bunk bed, feuding with our dorm's mold infestation, and rambling about our random pancake cravings late at night, into the early hours of the morning. A true roommate success story, if you will.

But I digress...

As Brené Brown eloquently shed light on in her TED Talk, vulnerability is universal. It's the idea that to form connections we have to allow ourselves to be really *seen*. And vulnerability serves as the foundation of shame.

"No one wants to talk about it, and the less you talk about it, the more you have it," Brené explained.[17]

---

17   Blackburn, Paul. 2018. "Brené Brown On The Power Of Vulnerability | Global Success Academy." *Global Success Academy.* https://theglobalsuccessacademy.com/brene-brown-ted-talk/.

This perception of vulnerability has similar origins to that of mental health. It is relevant to every person, but more often than not, no one really wants to talk about it.

Brené, a researcher who has dedicated twenty-plus years of her life to delving into concepts such as courage and empathy, was determined to grasp what it means to be vulnerable. Her year of investigation somehow turned into six years. She examined all participants in her study who displayed a sense of "worthiness" and found that what they shared was their ability to fully embrace their vulnerabilities.[18]

"They didn't talk about vulnerability being comfortable, nor did they really talk about it being excruciating—as I had heard earlier in the shame interviewing," Brené remarked. "They just talked about it being necessary."

"They talked about the willingness to say, 'I love you' first . . . the willingness to do something where there are no guarantees . . . the willingness to breathe through waiting for the doctor to call after your mammogram. They're willing to invest in a relationship that may or may not work out. They thought this was fundamental."

---

18   Ibid.

We humans live in a vulnerable world. And one way people tend to deal with this vulnerability is to numb it, at whatever cost. The problem is that you can't selectively and strategically rid yourself of a certain feeling, such as vulnerability. It would be convenient if you could, but it simply doesn't work like that.

"When we numb those, we numb joy, we numb gratitude, we numb happiness. And then we are miserable, and we are looking for purpose and meaning, and then we feel vulnerable," Brené added.

This notion of vulnerability can manifest in various ways, and it does not discriminate.

You may have heard of John Green, the author who enchanted young readers with his number-one bestseller, *The Fault in Our Stars,* later adapted into a movie that had viewers (equipped with popcorn, tissues, and chocolate) in tears all across the globe.

But back in his awkward middle school years, when braces were abundant and hormones were racing, Green was a victim of bullying. And he felt isolated and alone.

"Middle school is really, really painful. I didn't know how to make it stop, and I didn't feel like I had any ability to make it stop. And that was really scary," he admitted years later, looking back on this traumatic period of his adolescence.[19]

"For me, being bullied in middle school felt very much like this huge force that I could do nothing about. Like I couldn't fix the fact that I was a huge nerd, and I couldn't fix the fact that I didn't know how to talk to people in a way that made them like me. Or made them accept me. It felt like a math problem that I couldn't solve."

High school was also a trying time for Green, but for different reasons, as he wasn't a great student and had a lot of self-destructive impulses. At the time, he struggled with the sense that he could not control his own thoughts, but he found a way to channel these thoughts by writing about them in a book he later published: *Turtles All the Way Down* is an entire novel dedicated to Green's experiences with obsessive-compulsive disorder, commonly known as OCD.

"I wanted to try to find some direct expression for it if I could, so that I could show myself and the people I love in my own life not just what this feels like and how scary it can feel, but I wanted to try to give people a glance of what it is," Green explained.

19 McCandless Farmer, Brit. 2018. "John Green's Advice: Don't Forget To Be Awesome." *Cbsnews.Com.* https://www.cbsnews.com/news/john-green-advice-dont-forget-to-be-awesome-60-minutes/.

OCD is still something that Green battles today; it hasn't simply disappeared, but it seems that he has gained a much better grasp of it over time, in part by opening up and accepting his struggles with the disorder.

Green has become an active advocate for fostering healthy, honest discussions about mental health. When asked about the specifics of him being "weird" about food in a 60 Minutes interview, he replied, "I can't really talk about the specifics of it because I get squirmy. Because it's ongoing. It's not a dragon that I've slain. It feels very dangerous to talk about it.[20]

"It almost feels like if I start talking about it, then it might become *real*."

Additionally, at a recent book signing, Green openly announced to all his fans that he would unfortunately not be able to take pictures with any of them due to his OCD.

"It's not personal, but … I don't want to touch you," he confessed, addressing the crowd.

While it's definitely not easy and requires a considerable amount of time and effort, Green has found little ways to embrace his vulnerability, largely through his writing, which

---

20   Ibid.

appears to have contributed to his success as an author, producer, vlogger, and educator.

His honest takes and the raw emotions reflected in his work go a long way to build and capture a large (and eager) audience. Despite the fact that not all teenagers can directly relate to John Green's personal hardships, most have experienced some combination of loss, grief, and pain. Maybe the specifics of the experiences aren't universal, but the core emotions certainly are.

His overall advice? Be true to yourself and "don't forget to be awesome."

CHAPTER 3

LACK OF ADEQUATE RESOURCES

———

I was shaking.

Maybe it was from the latte I had chugged moments before, or maybe it was because there was a slight breeze and, of course, I had once again actively ignored the weather forecast (and my mother's best judgement) and failed to bring a jacket—or maybe it was just pure nerves.

I circled the parking lot once more and frustratingly pounded the "route" button on Google Maps. I'd always been directionally challenged and would undoubtedly be a goner on a survivalist game show within minutes.

On this rare occasion, I had managed to arrive not on time but *early*. What had come over me?

Finally, she picked up.

"Hello?"

"Hi, this is Ali Friedman . . . this is kind of awkward . . . I think I'm here, but I can't seem to figure out exactly which building you're located in. Are you next to the DSW?"

"Hey Ali. Yes, I'm by DSW."

"Great! I'll be right in—"

"Actually, I don't seem to have you on my calendar for today."

"Oh . . ."

"Could we maybe reschedule?"

"Uh yeah . . . sure," I muttered.

"Great. Just text me!"

"Will do."

I hung up the phone and sat idly in my ancient, beat-up minivan. Like a soccer mom with no destination—the game had been canceled.

Several months earlier, after countless panic attacks, sleepless nights, and self-imposed isolation in my tiny single dorm room, I had finally come to the realization that I needed to speak to someone.

Therapy had always been something we discussed in my psychology classes that I recognized as a valuable resource, but never one I had imagined I myself would need.

I don't know why the idea bothered me so much, as I am a huge proponent of self-care and mental health. But there I was: exhausted, anxious, and in my head. Not sure what was happening or where to go next.

Finally, now that it was summer, after much procrastination, I had emailed several therapists in the area to see if anyone was available. After going back and forth a couple times, this person and I had arranged to meet today, Monday, at 11 a.m. sharp.

At the time, I was working two different summer jobs. Monday was the only day I worked in Bethesda, Maryland, for the full 9–5 day, without changing locations. I had specifically requested an hour and a half off in the middle of the work day to make this initial appointment. The therapist had informed me that 11 a.m. on Monday was all she had available.

I continued to sit dejectedly in my minivan, listening to the hum of the engine, which sounded like it could break down at any moment.

Had I made a mistake on my end? Did we not agree to meet at 11 this morning? I quickly scrolled through my emails to find our prior conversation.

"**Let's plan on meeting this Monday at 11 a.m. I look forward to meeting you**," her response to me read.

I scrolled down to our most recent exchange:

"**That sounds great! I will see you on Monday at 11 a.m. Thank you so much!**" I had confirmed.

I checked the date on my calendar once again—*was I going crazy? Was today not Monday?*

Sure enough, it was Monday. Since I had already taken a little time off work and was right next to the mall, I decided to go ahead and treat myself to a croissant for my troubles.

My mom called me while I was about to head back to work.

"Hey honey! Sorry to bother you, but . . . wait a minute, aren't you supposed to be at your first appointment right now?"

I didn't have the heart to tell her that my therapist had canceled on me. After I had already arrived.

"I think there was some sort of mix-up. . . . It's been postponed until next week," I explained. I tried to hide the disappointment in my voice.

Fast-forward several months: It was now October. The leaves were starting to change color, despite it having been unusually cold. Almost as if Mother Nature had skipped right to winter. Some ambitious stores already had Thanksgiving decor and Christmas lights in their window displays.

My eyes were growing heavy from the dense piece of literature I was skimming for my history class. I half-heartedly glanced at my emails to see if there was anything urgent to respond to. Or any new sales at Urban Outfitters—also arguably urgent.

I had received an email with the subject line "Accepting New Patients?"

What? That must be a mistake. Who is this even from?

I clicked on it. It was a response to the initial email I had sent months earlier, when I was first inquiring about therapists in the area over the summer.

I double-checked the date of the initial email I had sent to make sure I hadn't gone crazy: July 2.

This email response was sent to me on October 3. **October 3.**

"Good afternoon Ali,

Thank you for reaching out to ——.

In order to get you scheduled, please contact me so I am able to conduct a brief phone intake.

We will need your insurance, date of birth, diagnosis (if any), reason for visit, any safety concerns, how did you hear about us, and scheduling availability.

Look forward to hearing back from you.

Regards."

I was floored. Absolutely no acknowledgement of the three months that had passed. Just a routine, almost robotic response. No fluff.

After the initial shock had subsided, I started getting heated.

Three months???

Again, I was shaking. But this time from pure anger.

Three months?! Why respond at all? Were they on vacation for three months? Without any sort of automated "out of the office" response message? Do they own a calendar? What century do they think this is?

While I sensed the annoyingly millennial tone of my thoughts, I couldn't suppress them.

I shut my laptop and went outside to get some fresh air, in a desperate attempt to calm myself down.

I'm just overreacting. It's not that big of a deal.

But it was no use.

I quickened my pace and trudged on.

Not even a chocolate croissant could fix this. I stopped briefly to hastily yank my sweatshirt off. Despite the fall breeze, I was sweating bullets. Physically upset.

Trembling and all, I felt my fingers moving a mile a minute as I furiously typed six texts in a row to one of my close friends, who I knew would get my frustration, as she too was familiar with logistical issues when it comes to booking an appointment with a therapist.

I grabbed my earbuds and aggressively turned up the volume of the rap music I so enjoyed, which usually hyped me up and lifted my spirits, regardless of what else was going on.

But even Kanye couldn't drown out my frustration. As he rapped about waves, the only thing going through my mind was that I had to fight off the urge to send an angry reply to the delayed response from this therapist. Despite my sudden surge of emotions, I had enough sense to know that would not get me anywhere.

Mental health is certainly not a joke.

But this situation was.

It had to be.

* * *

According to the National Alliance on Mental Illness, **75% of all mental health conditions begin by age twenty-four, and one in five young adults will experience a "mental health condition during college**."[21] These alarming statistics demonstrate the reality of how critical it is to foster an environment that promotes discussions about mental wellness during the college years in particular.

Furthermore, college campuses across the country seem to be in a mental health crisis of sorts, and the data doesn't point to an improvement anytime soon. Studies have shown that conditions such as anxiety, eating disorders, and depression are associated with lower GPAs and a higher likelihood of dropping out of university.

Many college students are unaware of the resources their university offers, and often those who do know about them feel "uncomfortable navigating treatment for a severely stigmatized issue," according to USA Today.[22] Unfortunately,

---

21 "Starting The Conversation | NAMI: National Alliance On Mental Illness." 2019. *Nami.Org.* https://www.nami.org/About-NAMI/Publications-Reports/Guides/Starting-the-Conversation.

22 Simon, Caroline. 2017. "More And More Students Need Mental Health Services. But Colleges Struggle To Keep Up." *Usatoday.Com.* https://www.usatoday.com/story/college/2017/05/04/more-and-more-students-need-mental-health-services-but-colleges-struggle-to-keep-up/37431099/.

counseling requires significant funding; even the college counseling centers partially subsidized by the university entail payment for appointments, putting students from a lower socioeconomic status at a huge disadvantage. And socioeconomic status aside, many students seeking help have felt the need to involve their parents because of the required costs—something not everyone feels comfortable doing.[23]

There has been an increase in demand for college counseling services, which has grown "at least five times faster than average student enrollment."[24] While it's somewhat encouraging that more students in recent years have felt they could reach out to their university's services for help, it is quite concerning that the average college resources have been largely unable to accommodate every student in need.

* * *

SLEEP: THE ALL-ENCOMPASSING CURE?

They say that sleep is the cure for everything: studying for a big exam? Get more sleep; it will help with memory

23   Ibid.
24   Beresin, Eugene. 2017. "The College Mental Health Crisis: Focus On Overall Wellbeing." *Psychology Today*. https://www. psychologytoday.com/us/blog/inside-out-outside-in/201703/ the-college-mental-health-crisis-focus-overall-wellbeing.

consolidation.[25] Want to lose weight? Get on a regular sleep schedule. Sick? Try to get a few extra Zs in. But getting eight hours of sleep and regularly going to bed and waking up at the same time each day is a textbook example of something much easier said than done. Enter life.

Meredith Valmon, a U.S. Olympian, pointed out that the mental health resources offered today—both at universities and elsewhere—are noticeably more extensive than what existed thirty years ago.

"I guess it wasn't really on my radar because I just felt like it was normal. I felt like it was normal and expected there," Meredith said in response to whether she noticed any detrimental effects to her peers due to the lack of awareness about mental health issues and institutions in place to counteract them.

She then launched into a story about a girl on the track team during her freshman year in college, which she repeatedly recounts to her kids to this day:

> She was on the track team with me and it
> was exam time, and I remember being at

25 Rasch, Björn, and Jan Born. 2013. "About Sleep's Role In Memory." *Pubmed Central*. doi:10.1152/physrev.00032.2012.

practice, she was saying she was so tired, and so I asked her, "Oh, well what's going on?"

She said, "Well, I got up at four in the morning to study."

So I thought, *Oh maybe this is some type of study technique where you wake up in the middle of the night and study for half an hour or an hour. It kind of solidifies the information in your brain; maybe you study intermittently throughout the night to just keep it going. This is interesting.* And she was pre-med, so she was super intense and super competitive, worrying about how she was going to get into med school even as a freshman.

When Meredith asked her teammate what time she usually goes back to sleep after getting up at four in the morning to study, she looked puzzled.

"What do you mean? I'm not going back to sleep until midnight tonight," she replied.

Meredith assumed that her teammate was practicing some sort of new study method to better retain information and was curious about how long the study sessions in the middle of the night needed to be in order to reap the benefits, but apparently that was not the case.

In reality, that was just the schedule this student felt she had to be on to get all of her schoolwork done. When Meredith realized her teammate was not engaging in a trendy study tactic and was actually waking up in the middle of the night to study for 20 hours a day, she was shocked.

"I kind of recognized that this was crazy," Meredith admitted. "But there's nothing to do with that, but just write it off and say, 'Well, this is what it's like to be pre-med at Harvard. I'm glad I'm not premed.'"

Needless to say, that was Meredith's teammate's last year on the track team. It is not terribly uncommon for college students to pull all-nighters, or to not consistently clock in the recommended eight hours of sleep each night.

In early 2016, the Huffington Post published an article titled *Is 'Sleep When You're Dead' Georgetown University's Unofficial Motto?* that had gained considerable attention since a couple of Georgetown students created a video highlighting the campus's unhealthy sleep culture two years prior.[26]

---

26 Gottfried, Sydney. 2017. "Is 'Sleep When You're Dead' Georgetown University's Unofficial Motto?" *Huffingtonpost.Com.* https://www.

Finding a balance and obtaining a sufficient amount of sleep in order to thrive and prosper is no easy feat.

How did Meredith achieve a balance between the pressures of an Ivy League university and simultaneously running competitively on her varsity team?

"It was really challenging. But I think they go together," Meredith explained. "It wouldn't have been really that different if I was there at Harvard just competing academically, because you have to do that. In this environment where you need to compete and do well, and you need to put in the work and figure out how to do that. So, for me, it was kind of like doing it on parallel tracks, the academic side and the athletic side, but I don't think it would have been any less intense doing only one."

While Meredith had been an athlete for her entire life and decided to run for her college team, she found it challenging to keep up with the rigorous academics while simultaneously competing at such a high level. But it was all about finding a balance. It made sense for her to pursue running as well as higher education, culminating in a degree, so she found ways to make it work.

---

huffingtonpost.com/sydney-jean-gottfried/is-sleep-when-youre-dead-_b_8917488.html.

"You just have to find a way to do both," Meredith mused. "In the bus on the way to the track meet, I'm getting ready to run in the meet. But I'm also doing my reading for my philosophy class. So it's in that moment, doing what I need to do—it's just instead of doing it for one thing, I'm doing it for two things at the same time."

* * *

"You can't control much of what goes on around you. Especially as a little kid. You have very little control over your own life. You certainly can't control what other people say or do and you don't really have any meaningful control over the adults in your life, but you always have control over your own mindset," Meredith emphasized to me.

It's true that, in life, there are many things outside of our control. That was a terrifying realization for me, one that fueled a panic attack while I was driving an extremely familiar route. It can be a hard reality to accept. But, as Meredith suggested, to some extent, promoting our mental health is within our realm of control.

Her overall advice is to be proactive about your well-being, rather than waiting until a serious problem arises that seems nearly insurmountable.

"It's always triggered by when something's starting to go wrong," she pointed out.

In some ways, it seems like the topic of mental health only enters the conversation when something is going wrong. Instead of just focusing on a period of particularly high stress, perhaps there is value in recognizing when you are doing really well too. Maybe three weeks ago you weren't stressed, but you didn't focus on the fact that you were doing a really great job managing your health at the time, and there are mechanisms—whether formal or informal—you may have used back then that could apply in your current scenario as well.

"This is something that people can learn at a really young age, that this is something that they're in control of," Meredith affirmed. "So I think we may associate it with being an adult, where something traumatic happens and you need therapy or, once you get to be an adult and you have a stressful career, then that's when you need to start working on your mental health. I think I would send the message that it's not something that you wait until you have a problem to deal with. It's kind of something that you should be managing all along, and I think we can teach children that from a young age."

For instance, Meredith didn't start seeing a sports psychologist until she felt like her anxiety about competing was really holding her back.

"Whereas, if I had maybe built it into my routine from earlier on, it might not have even ever become a problem. It should just be something that we teach people," she reemphasized.

Even in today's modern society, although people are starting to become more open about how they are doing and what challenges they might be facing, promoting mental wellness appears to be more retroactive than proactive.

It would be ideal if we started teaching people how to foster an environment in which they're able to monitor their well-being and intervene or make adjustments when they sense something going slightly awry. If we can start to educate people at an earlier age, some things are within our control to enhance our mental wellness.

Further, it would be beneficial for all of us to focus on equipping people from a young age with the tools necessary to be aware of their health and recognize when they need help, as well as to empower people to manage their own mental state as much as they can. Part of this process involves greater self-awareness and promulgating the idea that resources are available and there is always someone out there willing to talk to you and help you through whatever you're struggling with.

* * *

My discouraging experiences with trying to gain access to counseling resources when I was at my lowest and most vulnerable definitely set me back, given that it took me a while to gather up the strength to reach out for help in the first place. However, in a sense, my frustration propelled me to action.

After my own struggles trying to find an available therapist, I was finally able to reach out to a couple of my close friends to vent and blow off some steam. By doing so, I realized that I was not the only one who tried to reach out to counseling services and had trouble landing regular appointments with a therapist due to a lack of adequate staffing. While this added to my overall frustration, it helped knowing that I was not alone and not the only one running into roadblocks. In a way, this notion gave me the courage to continue fighting—not merely for my own sake, but for everyone else in need.

Something needed to be done about this.

The issue at hand is twofold: colleges today do not have the budget or ability to provide their students with sufficient access to mental health resources, and even when such services are provided, the stigma surrounding mental illness remains a significant barrier.

Between 2014 and 2015, half of college counseling centers did not hire new staff, and the centers' budgets did not change to match the increases in demand. At the University of Southern California, the waiting period for students seeking counseling is typically six to eight weeks.[27]

"It's awful. It's tough because at USC they're really understaffed and under-resourced," student Hannah Nguyen explained, calling on the school's administration to expand services.

Hannah was only able to bypass the waitlist after having suicidal thoughts and post-traumatic stress attacks after being sexually assaulted by another student at the university, according to *The Atlantic*.[28]

---

27 Kwai, *The Atlantic.*
28 Ibid.

CHAPTER 4

MOVING IN THE RIGHT DIRECTION

———

There it was. That tiny little "W" that stood out like a sore thumb on my transcript. Those microscopic sharp lines creating a letter that I was allowing to control my happiness. Weighing me down.

The letter "W" typically represents wins, and it's often used to hype up sports teams—like "let's get this W!" But this was certainly not a win in my book. Quite the contrary. It's not like I had never experienced failure before. But this felt more like defeat. That was something I wasn't accustomed to. Resignation.

The email my dean sent me was gently worded but to the point:

Dear Ali,

I was notified because the ACCT 101 exam
that you took recently was just graded. I'm
not sure if you have seen the grade yet. . . .
Because the ACCT 101 assessments were later
than usual, the dean's offices are allowing
students in the course to withdraw late
from the course in case they wanted to after
getting this grade. I'm not recommending
that you need to withdraw, but I wanted to
let you know that you have that option. If
you do wish to withdraw, you need to email
me to request it **no later than this Thursday**.
I'd be happy to meet with you before then to
discuss if that's helpful.

I was absolutely stunned. I had run out of time on the last
exam and rushed to scribble down some notes to show that
I had at least prepared, but I didn't even get a chance to fully
read over the questions toward the end. I knew I had done
poorly but, nevertheless, I wasn't prepared for this.

I still have the text message I painfully crafted to my group
members, which in retrospect was more like rambling than
a message:

"Hi! Ok this is gonna seem super random &
weird & I honestly really didn't see this coming
but long story short I'm withdrawing from
accounting. I met w my dean today and basically there's no way I could keep my double
major + the business minor it's just too many
credits that I physically don't have the space to
fill and I honestly wasn't doing great anyways
& since I was only in it for the business minor
it doesn't make sense for me to continue w it.

I totally didn't realize we still had 1 more
group project though and I feel really bad
about that so I can for sure still try to help
with that (although I'm sure I won't be that
useful haha) but otherwise I can def talk to
our prof and explain the situation to her to see
if it'd be possible for you to team up w someone else in the class cause I def don't wanna
like leave u guys in the dust or anything.

Again so sorry to spring this on you and sorry
that was an actual novel but I can def meet
w our professor to see if there's anything I
can do!!"

This was back in the spring of my junior year. I had made it three quarters of the way through the course already; all that was left was one more group project and the final exam. Having to back out of the last group project was what really cut deep. Letting myself down was one thing, but letting others down was a whole different ball game. I swore to never be that person—the group member who doesn't show up to the meetings, or contribute, or pull their weight. But there I was.

I will never forget the sinking feeling I had as I walked into my dean's office that afternoon to discuss my options moving forward. I had never met her before since she was new to the position; I was fighting to hold back tears and to force a weak attempt at a smile onto my face.

For the twenty minutes I was there, I kept wondering what she thought of me. I had to suppress the urge to stop myself from exclaiming, "I promise I'm not usually like this! I am not a quitter. I'm a good student. I work really hard, at least."

This wasn't just about accounting. It was about taking care of myself and stepping back to look at the bigger picture—as cheesy and cliche as that may sound.

Was I really going to let balance sheets tear me apart? Are debits and credits going to determine where I go from here?

I would like to think that under normal circumstances, I would've gotten through it. I would've had to sacrifice some sleep and some sanity, but that was nothing new: welcome to the life of an average college student.

I remember calling my mom after meeting with my dean and making the decision to withdraw from the course, the infamous Accounting 101. As soon as she answered the phone, she could tell that something was wrong by my quivering voice. Her immediate words of concern have stuck with me:

"Honey, what's going on? Are you okay?"

That's when I really broke down. I couldn't fool my mom— she is all-knowing, as many moms magically seem to be.

"Mom, please don't be mad at me. It's been really tough this semester. I . . . I . . . uh, really bombed this exam. I just don't think I can . . . do it anymore. I tried." My defense was up; I kept on trying to rationalize what had gone wrong. *Why was this such a low point for me?*

Although I had anticipated the worst, as usual, my fear was far worse than the reality. My mom reassured me that I was making the right decision, and that she was there for me.

But what was I going to tell my roommates? They were bound to notice the following Monday, when I would break my usual routine of grabbing a granola bar as I sprinted out the door at 9:25 a.m. to make it to my 9:30 accounting class. What would they think? What about all my friends who had previously gotten through accounting—would they judge me?

I ended up casually mentioning my withdrawing from the course in conversation with my four roommates, in sort of a passing, joking manner. Attempting to make light of the situation, as I often do when I am struggling. I felt that if I made it seem like it wasn't a big deal, maybe I would start to believe that myself.

People struggle; failure happens. It's all part of life. But this W was a pretty big turning point for me: I realized there must have been some underlying issues I was dealing with, that I could no longer keep to myself. It was about time I addressed my anxiety—I simply couldn't go on like this.

* * *

ART AS AN OUTLET FOR STRESS

"They have these experiences that aren't necessarily traumatizing, but they see the world in a light that's different from everyone else."

Before coming to Juilliard, Hannah Park, now a recent graduate, hadn't really had any close personal experiences with mental illness. While she was sure there were people who were suffering, she didn't know of anyone with mental health issues—or at least anyone who was open about it at the time. Once she got to college, it was a whole other story, and she was shocked by how common it was.

For those who don't know, the Juilliard School is a highly renowned performing arts conservatory in New York City. It is ranked first among global performing arts schools, with an acceptance rate that is often lower than 7%.

"I think just to be any kind of artist, whether you paint or act or dance or sing, it's like you have to be emotionally vulnerable and know what you're feeling inside to clearly express it in another form," Hannah explained.

One of Hannah's closest friends at Juilliard lost her mom when she was really young and had been on antidepressants for four or five years prior. In college, her depression became quite severe; she really had to be on top of tracking her medication, how it was making her feel, and whether it was the correct dosage. She had a difficult time her second year at school, and then decided to take a year off, but was open about the reason for her leave of absence and was later able to return to school. Although Hannah was cognizant of the importance of mental health, she had never really experienced something like this firsthand.

"I realized I was one of the few people in my class not on medication. I was like the only one in my class who hadn't been to counseling. Art attracts that kind of person more than any other professional field. It was interesting to be surrounded by people who had very different mindsets than I did," she elaborated.

Embracing your emotional vulnerability seems to be a key part of being an artist. A lot of dancers in particular use their art as a means of expressing themselves and the hardships they have endured, as in the case of Hannah's best friend coming to terms with the loss of her mother.

Hannah's experiences at Juilliard opened her eyes to the impact your surroundings can have and how a supportive community can make a big difference.

"I think it has a lot to do with the environment you're in," Hannah affirmed. "In high school, I never heard anyone talk about anything like that. No one wanted to even talk about any sort of personal experiences in health class or anything. It was totally different when I got to Juilliard. It was nice that they weren't shy about it."

While the change of surroundings took some getting used to, in a sense, Hannah found it refreshing to be around people who were confident and open about their issues; many of her classmates put themselves out there, proclaiming whatever they were going through and laying it all out on the table. They were true to themselves via the honesty through which they recognized their ongoing battles.

"A large majority of artists in every field lean towards art because it helps them relieve and express their life troubles. People use dance to talk about depression, or bipolar disorder, or people who feel suicidal. And that helps them relieve some of their stresses," Hannah emphasized.

Similarly, Annika Cowles highlighted how acting provides her with a space for self-expression, which can help alleviate some of the pressure she often experiences.

Annika mentioned, however, that many actors struggle with separating the identities of the characters they are playing from what they themselves are going through.

"We're all constantly talking about how we're feeling, but it's easier to talk about other people's issues than our own," Annika admitted. "We talk a lot about our characters and how they're feeling. It's always about how your character is feeling, but not so much about how you're feeling."

It can sometimes be tricky to differentiate between the perspective of a character you're playing versus your personal feelings. Annika added that sometimes actors engage in method acting, which involves using their character as an excuse for certain behavior—certainly not a healthy practice.

"I think rejection in my work life is easier to handle than in my personal life. With work I can just be like, 'Okay, that wasn't my best audition,' but I take friend drama or a guy rejecting me a lot harder than roles. Just because I haven't spent that much time on myself, or time analyzing those areas where I think I need to," Annika illustrated.

Additionally, therapy is seen as a valuable resource at the University of the Arts, but the university itself does not seem to offer sufficient on-campus resources for its students. Most of Annika's classmates are in some sort of therapy or counseling and go to private therapists off campus.

"We take care of that for the characters, but for ourselves we're not given those same resources," Annika told me. "Almost all my friends go to therapy as well as physical therapy, but it's not offered through the school."

While Annika's university does provide some counseling services, the school's physical therapist is only available for dance majors. While it's logical that the students who dance would need access to physical therapy, Annika pointed out that actors are also constantly moving around, and it's not uncommon for an actor to pull a muscle.

"Our bodies are literally our instruments," she said.

The college students of today seek out counseling services on campus more often than "any other generation in the modern history of the United States," according to *The Atlantic*, and the vast majority of said students cite anxiety and depression as their primary concerns.[29] While it is somewhat encouraging that students are becoming more open to getting help when needed, there's no evidence that college students of past generations did not face the same mental-health struggles— only that they were far less commonly discussed or addressed.

In 2004, Congress signed the Garrett Lee Smith Memorial Act, which channels millions of dollars into suicide-prevention research, including early-intervention programs. Since it was signed into law, schools across the country have become more in tune to the mental health issues their students are confronting.[30]

"When students are in treatment, they are far less likely to be at risk," Ben Locke, executive director of the Center for

29   Kwai, *The Atlantic*.
30   Ibid.

Collegiate Mental Health, stated. "In the last decade, we have been telling students, parents, roommates, friends, if you see somebody who is struggling, refer them to service."

Although some view the jump in students taking advantage of their school's resources positively, for others, particularly college administrators, this increased demand has sparked a fear that students are becoming "more sensitive and less resilient," which has fueled a heated debate on the national stage.[31]

The reality is that this is largely a dangerous misconception; the fact that more students are reaching out for help does not mean that today's college students are in any way less "resilient." Locke emphasized that the fear that students have suddenly lost their coping skills is unfounded, and he pointed to evidence that "large-scale changes in national policy and culture over the last decade have, in fact, worked," *The Atlantic* reported.[32]

* * *

---

31 Gray, Peter. 2015. "Declining Student Resilience: A Serious Problem For Colleges". *Psychology Today*. https://www.psychologytoday.com/us/blog/freedom-learn/201509/declining-student-resilience-serious-problem-colleges.

32 Kwai, *The Atlantic*.

"We want you to take a break, relax, get yourselves together, and don't come up here—to be hyperbolic about it—don't come up here borderline suicidal because you've been driving yourself so hard for four, five, six, seven, eight years to get into a school like this."

When Meredith's son Travis was accepted to Harvard, he received a three-and-a-half page letter in his incentives package, outlining all the benefits of taking a gap year before starting university. Harvard made it very clear that he had been accepted and could enroll that upcoming fall if he so chose, but also that he had the option of taking a year off before attending. Such a letter was not unique to Travis: it has become a standard part of the Harvard admissions packet to include a lengthy explanation of why the school would like you to consider taking a gap year, along with the acceptance letter.[33]

On Harvard's website, the article "Time Out or Burn Out for the Next Generation," details the effects of early sources of pressure in our educational system:

33 Strauss, Valerie. 2016. "Why Harvard 'Encourages' Students To Take A Gap Year. Just Like Malia Obama Is Doing.". *Washington Post*. https://www.washingtonpost.com/news/answer-sheet/wp/2016/05/01/why-harvard-encourages-students-to-take-a-gap-year-just-like-malia-obama-is-doing/?utm_term=.7ef03825a39d.

Faced with the fast pace of growing up today, some students are clearly distressed, engaging in binge drinking and other self-destructive behaviors. Counseling services of secondary schools and colleges have expanded in response to greatly increased demand. It is common to encounter even the most successful students, who have won all the "prizes," stepping back and wondering if it was all worth it. Professionals in their thirties and forties — physicians, lawyers, academics, business people and others — sometimes give the impression that they are dazed survivors of some bewildering life-long boot-camp. Some say they ended up in their profession because of someone else's expectations, or that they simply drifted into it without pausing to think whether they really loved their work. Often they say they missed their youth entirely, never living in the present, always pursuing some ill-defined future goal.[34]

"I think they are trying to say, 'Look, we don't want to have an entire class of stressed-out, burnt-out kids,'" Meredith

---

34 Ibid.

offered. "They're like, 'Look, take a break, take a rest, deal with some of this before you come here. We want to be equipped to help people in this environment, but we also would love if more people would come less burnt-out.'"

Harvard's efforts to encourage students to consider taking some time off before enrolling reveal how crazy and stressful the college process has become and that elite colleges have begun to recognize the toll it has taken on prospective admits. The admissions process has in general continued to become more competitive, as the number of applicants rises across the board.

"The part that really stands out in my mind was where it said, 'Do not feel like you need to spend this year doing anything to impress us. If you're accepted, you're admitted—you've done it, you're in, you might just need to spend this year reading some books and reconnecting with your family.' And, to me that was a glaring siren," Meredith recalled. "They were saying, 'You guys are too stressed out.' That's why I say I think it even starts before kids get on campus now to address this mental wellness issue. So I am certain that once you're there, it also is something being actively addressed."

Harvard's prompting students to think about taking a break before enrolling seems to be part of a broader recognition of what students go through to gain admission to a school like that with a 6% acceptance rate. While elite schools obviously can't eradicate the competition of the admissions process altogether, since they can only accept so many students, they are recognizing their position on the back end of that and consequently working to alleviate some of that pressure.

The vast majority of U.S. universities continue to encourage more and more people to apply for admission, by reducing the number of required essay questions, waiving application fees, and employing massive marketing campaigns.

Decades of economic theory have suggested that having more choices is always preferable, but recent research undermines this idea. The percentage of students applying to seven or more colleges has been growing exponentially.[35] Although having more options may seem desirable, evidence shows that students who apply to a greater number of universities, and hence have more choices, may experience a decline in intrinsic motivation. People are more likely to take on voluntary class essay assignments when offered a range of six choices rather than twenty-four or thirty choices.[36]

---

35 Soodik, Nicholas. 2017. "High School Students Are Applying To Too Many Colleges (Essay) | Inside Higher Ed." *Insidehighered.Com*. https://www.insidehighered.com/admissions/views/2017/12/04/ high-school-students-are-applying-too-many-colleges-essay.

36 Iyengar, Sheena, and Mark Lepper. 2000. "When Choice Is Demotivating: Can One Desire Too Much Of A Good Thing?" *Journal Of Personality And Social Psychology*. https://faculty.washington.edu/ jdb/345/345%20Articles/Iyengar%20%26%20Lepper%20(2000).pdf.

Furthermore, studies conducted by two social psychologists confirmed that having more choices can also reduce students' resulting satisfaction and amplify the regret they feel.[37] This phenomenon of choice overload is important for future high school students to consider when creating their list of schools to apply to.

But one factor driving seniors to apply to more and more colleges stems from the way modern culture frames college as a consumer product. This portrayal of university as a commodity suggests to students that applying to a greater number of colleges will maximize their chances of getting accepted to one that's the best fit for them.[38]

Buzzwords such as "fit" and "well-rounded" are often used by college admissions offices to give applicants the illusion that there is one specific school that will fit them seamlessly, but they underemphasize the selectivity of the institution.[39]

Meredith added that, although Harvard's disclosure of the benefits of taking a gap year is admirable, "on the flip side, they are actively trying to make it more competitive. I

---

37 Soodik, *Insidehighered.Com.*

38 Ibid.

39 Barnard, Brennan. 2019. "Six Terms To Stop Using In College Admissions." *Forbes.Com.* https://www.forbes.com/sites/brennanbarnard/2019/01/11/six-terms-to-stop-using-in-college-admission/#3af6d3391aed.

definitely got that message also during the admissions process. They encourage everybody. If you go to an information session there—the room is packed. I can't say how many people are in there, probably 300 kids. And they do that four times a day."

Schools want to brag that their applicants have the highest test scores and that they have the highest numbers applying, to increase the prestige and desirability of the school and to attract even more applicants.

"It's all about that elusive acceptance rate. Driving it even lower so they're working on one end to continue to make it more competitive. Not that even if they didn't say that it would be less so, but they're actively driving it and encouraging people to apply, knowing that 95% of them are going to get rejected," Meredith pointed out. "And then as you said, dealing with what it takes to make yourself the type of student that can get accepted.

"I feel like for them it must be kind of a ticking time bomb, having that level of stress that is produced in the process of getting in. So I kind of think they're working both ends of it."

Meredith by no means intends to single out Harvard specifically, but it's a school she is personally familiar with, having attended university there, sat in on a recent information session, and seen her son's acceptance package only a couple years back.

"I can speak to one school in particular, but I think this goes on all over the place; [Harvard is] not the only school trying to drive down their acceptance rate. Everything I'm saying could be said about half the schools in the country," Meredith stressed.

When Meredith ran at Harvard, hardly anyone—athletes and non-athletes alike—ever openly discussed their mental health. While including a couple of pages on the benefits of a gap year certainly does not alleviate the root cause of stress in the college admissions process, this adjustment serves as a positive step forward and appears to be a move in the right direction.

"Probably a lot of people are coming in already past burnt," Meredith explained. "You only have so much to work with because you've already done so much to be in a position to get accepted, and then you just have that short break between when you graduate and when you start up again. I don't think it's enough time to just kind of relax and read and restore yourself."

You don't have to be an aspiring Olympian to benefit from Meredith's experiences. There is a lot to be said for breaking a hefty vision or dream into smaller, more manageable pieces, to make your goal more attainable. And there's absolutely nothing wrong with taking a break—whether that's a year-long break between college and graduate school, a semester off from an extracurricular activity, or a quick pause from working at the office to get some fresh air and take a walk around the block to clear your head.

* * *

To this day, I still feel humiliated by my failed Accounting 101 experience. A lot of my friends are in the business school at Georgetown and had to take the exact same course freshman year. Few people enjoyed the class, but it was a requirement that many had to complete. A stepping stone. And they were able to get through it. Last month, the one time I was able to finally drag myself to the gym, one of my accounting group members happened to pass by my treadmill; naturally, I avoided eye contact and picked up the pace—fulfilling the literal definition of running away from my problems.

While the wound is still somewhat fresh, I've come a long way since that dreaded meeting with my dean. Failure happens, and this particular failure was the extra push I needed to get my priorities straight and address the anxiety issues I had attempted to ignore.

Despite what I've learned in every psychology class I've taken and my compassion for those with mental health issues, that darned stigma was still buried somewhere inside me, along with the anxious thoughts keeping me up at night that I had tried (and ultimately failed) to suppress. As cognizant and open-minded as I thought I was about mental illness, I, like many others, never thought it would actually happen to me. The last thing I wanted to be perceived as was weak in any way, shape, or form.

After months of vaguely considering making an appointment with a therapist, I finally took measures into my own hands and took that first step. Although that was not the end of my journey, it was a much-needed step in the right direction. My dean helped me realize that the added stress from accounting was by no means necessary: I was a government and psychology double major, had enough IB and AP credits to graduate early if I wanted to, had studied abroad to explore my interest in international relations, had board positions for two on-campus organizations, and was also trying to, you know, have a life.

What was I doing in accounting in the first place?

I had absolutely zero interest in the subject; I only registered for the course because it was required for the business minor, which I had been accepted to after a competitive application process.

But did I even want to go into business? Does a minor even matter?

The whole purpose of adding the business minor was to keep my options open. But my attempt to make my life more manageable further down the road had spurred the complete opposite outcome.

This is the sort of student mindset Project LETS aims to combat.

Project LETS is a nonprofit with ten chapters across the country dedicated to providing a peer-led community support network for college students battling mental illness. The organization aims to make mental health care more accessible for students in need while simultaneously training students who have experienced mental illness to equip themselves with the necessary tools to move forward.

"Project LETS is creating student networks of support and advocacy, rather than relying on already unreliable campus services or expensive and inaccessible off-campus aid," *The Nation* reported.[40]

Stefanie Kaufman founded Project LETS while she was in high school after her friend Brittany took her own life. As the community grieved the loss of Brittany, Stefanie was taken aback by the school district's failure to address the issue at hand, as it attempted to entirely sweep Brittany's death under the rug, fearing that any sort of dialogue about her suicide could trigger other students.[41] A group of high school students advocated bringing in suicide-prevention experts to speak to the student body, but their efforts were repudiated by the school.

"It was my first real introduction to being like, 'Wow, the educational system doesn't know how to handle this or address this,'" Stefanie recalled in an interview with *The Nation*. "I remember a memorial event was organized for her [outside of school]. And just getting together with other people who were grieving this loss in a collective space and sharing stories and just being present was what we really needed to heal and process. And that's exactly what our schools were trying to prevent."

40 Thorne, Gabriela. 2018. "Mental-Health Care On College Campuses Is Broken—This Group Aims To Change That". *The Nation*. https://www.thenation.com/article/mental-health-care-on-college-campuses-is-broken-this-group-aims-to-change-that/.

41 Ibid.

Through its research, the nonprofit has found significant differences in the requirements for students who are physically ill versus those who take psychiatric leave, in terms of time restrictions. Consequently, Project LETS worked with campus services to provide feedback about wait times and specific issues consistently arising with protocol on campus. The organization's advocacy led to Brown University hiring a crisis counselor who is now available for walk-in appointments for students.

"I think a lot of the conversation with mental health tends to center around experts," Stefanie pointed out. "I think people are often scared of having mentally ill people share their stories. Like, they may say the wrong thing or trigger someone. . . . But it's absolutely critical to see people with lived experiences as experts of what they go through and allow them spaces to share."

Project LETS holds workshops in which real students sit on a stage and share their personal stories about their illnesses, with a typical turnout of sixty to seventy students. They've found that students yearn to have a space where they can hear people "echoing what they go through," according to Stefanie.[42]

---

42   Ibid.

Project LETS' efforts have proven quite successful; over 70% of students involved with the program felt more prepared to handle crises afterward. Furthermore, the nonprofit has effectively increased access to resources among diverse racial, gender, and cultural groups and those from marginalized communities, since it is able to pair students based on shared aspects of their identity, at students' request.

College is a cauldron of changes. Learning to live with a stranger (often being thrown into an intimate setting), leaving the comforts of home, advocating for yourself, making friends, keeping up with academics, taking on new experiences, doing things outside of your comfort zone—it's all a lot to process.

College students often find themselves in no man's land—between adolescence, when you're under parental control, but before real adulthood, when you're completely independent. What is the college's responsibility, what is the student's, and what is the parents' role regarding their child's mental well-being?

CHAPTER 5

DON'T BE AFRAID TO ASK FOR HELP

———

"I'm tired of looking at dead kids."

Back in 2001, Derek Gaunt was working on another murder investigation. The girl was three years old at the time of her tragic death, and she visited Derek in his dreams for years after the event.

"This one affected me the most because at this point, I said, 'You know what—I don't even know if I want to be doing this anymore,'" he described. There are only so many murders a person can take.

In retrospect, Derek admitted he did not fully take advantage of the critical incident stress management (CISM) resources available to him when he was working on this case in particular. It was not until he later participated in a leadership school program that he started to reflect on and vocalize past moments in his life when he felt that he had "screwed up," or when something distressing happened that he internalized but never really came to terms with. Because of this program, the three-year-old girl finally stopped appearing in his dreams—after he was finally able to open up and share that traumatic experience in a group setting.

"There are people who are part of hostage negotiations teams now, as I speak, that are only there because, you know, they get to wear the shirt that says negotiator on it, or you get a front row seat at the sexiest game in town," Derek described. "When a hostage-taking or a barricaded event occurs, I don't care what city it's in, it sucks up a lot of resources. And as a negotiator, you get a front-row seat to that action.

"But **it's not a game.** That's what I tell them all the time."

Derek's mantra was brought into focus once again at an event back in 2005. Derek had just brought six brand new negotiators onto the team, who had practically "jumped up and down" at the opportunity. That day was significant because it was the first time in his career that he had six new team members who either heard or witnessed the shooting of the guy they were dealing with.

"It all came flooding home for them at that moment," Derek recalled. "That, you know, this is real stuff. This is not 'Because we're a small city it's never going to happen here; I'm just a part of a negotiating team.' This is real stuff.".

The novice team members either watched the shooting on a monitor, witnessed it up close, or listened to it over the phone. Being in the right mindset and then being provided an opportunity to fully express what they were going through after the fact proved crucial.

In another barricade event, Derek recounts the anger one of his negotiators expressed over the fact that "she had spent over ten hours on the phone with this guy, and then she had to be relieved. And then when another negotiator from another agency took over for her, within five minutes, the guy shot himself. And she was furious at this guy. She was furious at herself."

She kept questioning herself and agonizing over what she had not picked up on, what she had missed, and why she was not able to predict it would end that way. For her, it was helpful to have a CISM debrief after the event, so the rest of her team could hear what she was going through and share a different perspective with her.

"I want my team members to understand that every time your phone goes off alerting you to an event, when you come home that night, somebody may not be alive," Derek explained. "Somebody could die as a result of this incident. So if you don't get your head around that and approach your work and training with that mindset, you're going to contribute to the possibility of that happening."

Derek emphasized that some negotiators seem motivated by the wrong reasons—predominantly by the seemingly thrilling and risky nature of the work.

"I don't want those people around me. Because it's not a game," he reiterated.

Derek's sobering experiences as a hostage negotiator have taught him that this career is not one to be taken lightly, as many of these cases are a matter of life and death. There is not much room for error or joking around, so it is critical that all the training and preparation for these investigations are taken seriously and protocol is followed.

Due to the nature of the work, it can be challenging—for both newcomers and experienced leaders such as Derek—to cope with and recover from such traumatic incidents, and the value of teamwork and the CISM resources is evident. Ultimately, being able to open up and share disturbing experiences relieved hostage negotiators of some of their prolonged anguish and helped them move forward.

Similarly, though in a very distinct field, Meredith Valmon was able to reap the benefits of the resources available to her during her athletic career. It was not until she reached the world championship stage, however, that these services were offered.

"You're either strong or you're not"—up until relatively recently, that mentality appeared to dominate throughout the United States.

Meredith took a break from running between seventh grade and college, which was primarily to escape from some of the pressure she was under from running competitively at such a young age. While the specific phrase "mental health" was not commonly used at the time, the reason for Meredith's temporary departure from the sport was to focus on her mental wellness.

"Back in that era, you didn't really hear that phrase a lot," Meredith remarked. Mental health has become so much more—a catchphrase now where it's so much more common.

Maybe they talked about it in other ways back then, but I don't think so. I think it was more like this is life. You deal with it."

When she was in college, Meredith does not recall being informed that she had access to a psychologist. When asked if she knows where she would have gone if she felt like she had an issue, she responded by saying she supposed she would have tried to go to the student health center, but that had not really crossed her mind.

"I honestly don't even know where it was. I don't think I was even going there for physical illness, let alone would it have been made obvious to me that I could go there for any type of mental health issue. And I just mean mental wellness, even; I don't mean mental health, like a clinical diagnosis," she clarified.

There was one instance in particular when Meredith remembered feeling stressed out during her college years. Instead of going to the student health center, she made an appointment with another doctor in the area. When the doctor asked Meredith what was going on with her, she explained to him that she had a lot going on with her schoolwork and running, and that she was feeling overwhelmed trying to manage everything while getting only four hours of sleep a night.

"He said, 'I think that is probably at the root of a lot of what is going on with you,'" Meredith recalled. "And he sort of put it in my head, that if I could deal with my stress better, he didn't think that I would have some of these physical problems as well."

While the doctor did vaguely allude to the mental component of Meredith's problem, he did not refer her to another professional to try to address it. He casually mentioned that if Meredith needed to talk about her condition more, then she could come back and make another appointment.

"I think that would be very different nowadays," Meredith reflected. "And no one provided you with resources to manage being at a really academically competitive school and at the same time trying to compete at a national level in a sport. It was just expected to manage it."

"My coach was kind to the extent that if I went and said, 'I pulled an all-nighter and I have so much work to do,' he would say, 'Okay, skip practice, go home, get some rest, do your work.' That was the most I got. I never got any type of other techniques. It was just, 'find a way to get it done.'"

The stigma surrounding the concept of mental health still exists today. There are people in most societies who continue to view symptoms of psychopathology as "threatening and uncomfortable," which often leads to discrimination against those who suffer from mental illness.[43] What is particularly interesting and somewhat surprising is that these stigmatizing beliefs are not held by a particular subset of the population, but rather by a wide range of people, including family members of those with mental disorders.

According to a study of adolescents with mental health disorders, the aforementioned stigma came from teachers, peers, and family members alike:

> 46% of the adolescents described experiencing stigmatization by family members in the form of unwarranted assumptions . . . distrust, avoidance, pity and gossip. 62% experienced stigma from peers which often led to friendship losses and social rejection, and 35% reported stigma perpetrated by teachers and school staff, who expressed fear, dislike, avoidance, and under-estimation of abilities.[44]

---

43   Davey, *Psychology Today.*
44   Ibid.

The mental health stigma is even widespread in the medical profession, at least in part because it is given a low priority during the training of physicians and GPs.[45]

In short, mental illness used to be thought of primarily as a weakness or an excuse more than anything else, and it was simply not discussed. There was no recognition that it's good to be aware of your mental as well as physical health. Although improvements have been made, to some extent this stigma and misunderstanding about the realities of mental health are still prevalent today.

By the time Meredith got into the professional ranks, the topic of mental health had started to emerge. There was a greater focus on the mental side of the sport, but it still wasn't referred to as mental health.

"Then they were more aware that this is a huge part of it—how our athletes do is a huge part of it. So they got it and they said, 'We are going to make resources available; we are going to inform you that this is something you need to work on.' We called it sports psychology back then," she explained.

Meredith recalled that when she was on a world championships team, they were accompanied by a sports psychologist

45   Wallace, Jean. 2017. "Mental Health And Stigma in the Medical Profession." *Sage Journals*. doi:10.1177/1363459310371080.

whose main role was to teach the athletes how to operate in the maximally beneficial mental "zone" for the sport. Having access to a sports psychologist was certainly beneficial, but that didn't happen until she was in her twenties, predominantly due to her participation on the national team.

"Because I was at that level—national team level—I had other resources available to me even when I wasn't on the team. I went out to the Olympic Training Center in Chula Vista, in the San Diego area, and I trained there for a month, and there I got to see the sports psychologist."

When Meredith competed on the national team, it was encouraged but not mandatory to take advantage of having a sports psychologist on staff. Eventually, Meredith met with the psychologist to address the anxiety she had been experiencing with regard to her racing performance.

"It wasn't really for just my mental health, it was 'You're on the national team, and we need you to perform, and we know this is part of it.' But it was so that I could do well for the team. Not, 'This is something everybody should be doing for themselves,'" Meredith elaborated. "And now I would say over the past twenty years or so it has permeated so much more and gotten all over society and age groups and outside of sports obviously. I mean all of that was completely just related to sports. So it has changed a lot since then."

"One of the greatest benefits I got out of using the sport psychology services was where they explained to me the brain chemistry and what's going on in your brain when you feel certain things. And an issue I dealt with was anxiety and being nervous about how I would do and still dealing with that stress issue and the pressure of trying to make teams and do well and how to get into big international meets and trying to win a medal."

Many of the misconceptions about mental disorders are largely based on the fact that they are not as clearly visible as physical impairments, and they can be harder to grasp and define. But while these illnesses are classified under the "mental" realm, there is an actual biological groundwork for them as well. For example, it is often said that depression is caused by a chemical imbalance in the brain. Depression can result from "faulty mood regulation by the brain, genetic vulnerability, stressful life events, medications, and medical problems. It's believed that several of these forces interact to bring on depression," according to Harvard Health Publishing.[46] Mental health disorders such as depression can be more challenging to fully understand than physical ailments, since they are complex and can't be traced back to one specific origin alone.

---

46 Publishing, Harvard. 2009. "What Causes Depression? - Harvard Health". *Harvard Health*. https://www.health.harvard.edu/mind-and-mood/what-causes-depression.

"I think when I learned how it works, what's going on in my brain when I was feeling certain ways, that helped me understand it better and come up with, with the sports psychologist, some techniques that helped me manage it better," Meredith explained.

When it comes down to it, managing the mental aspect of your performance, like anything else, improves with practice over time.

"It's just like you practice physically. It's not something that someone tells you, 'This is what you do' and then that's it. You do have to work on it. It's really hard," Meredith admitted. "You have to work on it. So getting into a routine and trying different things and learning what seems to work better and discovering things I could tell myself that were effective and trying to be disciplined about saying those things—doing those things helps."

For Meredith, it was beneficial to think of both the physical and mental sides of running as one complete package that helped her prepare for races, as opposed to separating the two aspects from each other.

"That was my career; it was just all part of me doing my job— managing the mental side along with the physical side. And I would say for the mental side, a lot of it had to do with doing what I needed to do physically so if I knew, 'I'm doing the right workouts, I'm doing them well, I've worked hard, I feel good about them, I did everything'—that was what gave me the most peace of mind and helped me manage the mental aspect better. They just went so hand-in-hand for me," she described.

Meredith personally has noticed some tangible differences between how mental health was regarded when she was growing up and how it is perceived and treated today. Now, at her daughter's high school, it is a priority to not only provide mental health services, but also to teach the students the importance of their mental health and how to keep an eye on it. Her school district has begun to stress techniques and resources available to students if they need them, as well as symptoms to watch out for in their friends.

"I think now it's a much bigger part of life and athletics at younger ages," Meredith observed. "Mindfulness is a huge schoolwide, systemwide initiative now, where they have a special program in the morning. I think they call it the 'chill zone,' where you can come for fifteen minutes and learn to meditate before you start your day, and it's built into the school day, even at the middle school and, I would imagine, at the elementary school level also."

* * *

Similarly, Doug Grant has experience working in established settings, from Booz Allen Hamilton to his service in the U.S. Navy. While he believes that a stigma still exists surrounding mental health, the Navy in particular has become more equipped to tackle mental health issues. For example, Navy flight briefs now include standard questions addressing stress and overall well-being, to ensure that the pilots are in the right frame of mind before flying.

"I've actually done a lot of research and work with aviation mishaps. There are different levels of accidents. Obviously the worst is if you have a loss of life or a destroyed aircraft. And so they've put in a lot of controls with doing a brief beforehand, you know, talking about, 'Are you stressed at home?' That's part of a standard navy flight brief now. 'Did you get enough sleep? What's going on?' So everybody does pre-briefs beforehand," Doug explained.

Although this is one isolated example of a check the Navy has put in place, according to Doug's research and experience in the field, these Navy flight briefs have significantly lowered the mishap rates.

One of Doug's friends, a helicopter pilot, was on deployment when his fiancée broke things off with him. Naturally, he was not in a good place, and it was a devastating experience for him.

"They gave him several weeks where it was just like, 'Yeah, you're not flying.' Because they acknowledged that he wasn't in a mental space to do it. So I think because the job is more high risk, we're probably a little more tuned into it than the rest of the American workforce," Doug pointed out. "If you were a civilian doing a job, I don't think you could—partially because it's not like life or death circumstances—but you're not going to be going to your boss and saying, 'Hey, I've got these things going on' and be able to get as much leeway. So I think, at least from the aviation community, we actually do a pretty good job of that."

Booz Allen, where Doug serves as a product manager and consultant, performs periodic mental health checks and strives to prioritize mental health and treat it on an equal level as physical health. One physical measure Booz Allen has implemented is a Fitbit challenge among employees, to encourage them to get more exercise.

"So we do a Fitbit challenge, and if we hit a certain number of steps, we get like $200 or $300 in our health savings accounts. And they actually have a similar program for the mental health check. It's like some questions you answer and some surveys you do and you go through the process, assessing your mental health," Doug described. "They actually pay you to do it. So they're treating it the same as your physical health and giving the incentives for employees to do it. So it's a pretty big program. Booz is really, really good about it."

CHAPTER 6

FINDING WHAT WORKS FOR YOU

———

There is often a significant discrepancy between the access to mental health resources available in a large, established company compared to those available in a smaller business setting. While Doug Grant appreciates the resources offered by established entities like the U.S. Navy and Booz Allen Hamilton, he can also speak to the other side of the spectrum, as an early-stage startup founder.

After serving in the Navy for ten years, Doug pursued his MBA at Georgetown University. During his time at Georgetown, he founded Hemeos, a health care startup, and led a five-person team to develop the idea from concept to market in the highly regulated health care industry.

"I went through that whole crazy experience with the startup, which was definitely high stress," Doug recalled. "A different kind of stress from the Navy. I guess I had stress in all of those jobs. But yeah, flight school and the navy were definitely stressful. There's about a 30–40% dropout rate; you're constantly being evaluated as you fly. But running a startup was also stressful in its own right."

Running a startup is its own ballgame, with a host of unexpected challenges at every turn. When Doug created Hemeos, it was a completely different situation from the established settings he had previously worked in because he was primarily focusing on trying to get the company off the ground.

With startups, you don't really "have the bandwidth to have any sort of mental health programs for anybody. That was certainly a different kind of stress," he reiterated.

Similarly, Mitch Henkin, a small-business owner, is well aware of the challenges that come with a small-scale company, as opposed to a more established one.

Mitch worked as a sports writer for the *Washington Post* for five years before switching gears and founding TenniStar Sports. At the *Post*, Mitch recalled, employees were taught how to act in high-stress situations.

On the other hand, TenniStar is a company that runs sports camps during the summer. While Mitch is a master of tennis, his camp programs have expanded over the years to encompass field hockey, soccer, basketball, and lacrosse as well. In addition to running TenniStar, Mitch is the director of the Promenade Tennis Club, where he serves as the head tennis instructor and gives lessons daily. At the end of each and every day, ultimately the responsibility falls on his shoulders, which allows him to exert greater control to some extent, but also comes with its drawbacks.

While extremely passionate about tennis and eager to share his skill with others, Mitch runs the risk of spreading himself too thin. The sports camp business has been around since 1984 and has been largely successful. It can be a difficult enterprise to manage, as the primary camp season is during the summer, so there are high turnover rates among his staff members due to the seasonal nature of the camp business.

Mitch oversees countless staffers with complex and varying schedules, especially over the summer season. Managing the number of employees needed to adequately staff and instruct each camp without the formal mechanisms in place at larger companies is quite a feat. As a small business, TenniStar has no formal human resources department, for example.

Furthermore, smaller companies such as TenniStar lack the funds, manpower, and ability to offer mental wellness programs, so what are some more informal ways to promote success, regardless of whether you have access to resources offered in established company settings?

* * *

GIVE YOURSELF A BREAK

Take a break. Take a breather. Take five. Take a deep breath.

Words young children anxiously wait to hear while they are diligently practicing their piano pieces. Or what your coach tells your team when they want you to rest for five minutes before reconvening. Or perhaps the advice your teacher gives you to calm your nerves before a class presentation.

A plethora of meanings that all suggest the same thing: give yourself a little time to reset and recharge, whatever the context may be.

Meredith Valmon, now an American Olympian, initially started seriously running when she was eight years old.

"When I first started running, I didn't realize that there was a professional career doing it, but when I was little I did know about the Olympics, and I had a goal of making it to the Olympics one day," Meredith admitted.

Despite her lofty goal, Meredith actually took a break from the sport for about five or six years.

"From seventh grade to freshman year in college I didn't participate, so it wasn't a continuous thing," she explained. "And then, when I went back to it, I guess I was older, so I had more of an awareness that not everybody is going to make the Olympics. So my goals at that time were much more immediate."

When asked why she decided to temporarily leave the sport, Meredith responded that while she didn't really think about it in the moment, looking back, it had a lot to do with mental health and stress—although it would've been phrased in different terms at the time.

By the time she turned twelve, Meredith had already been running pretty seriously for four years, training several times a week almost year-round, as her season spanned from September through the end of July. She was traveling all over the country to compete at high-level meets and eventually got to the point where the sport became more stressful than fun.

"I'm a kid—this shouldn't feel like a job," Meredith remembered thinking. *"I should be trying different things. I shouldn't just be stuck on this one path; I want to do other things, like play an instrument, or act in a school play, or try a different sport.* I didn't want to pigeonhole myself."

Meredith's hiatus from running was motivated by a desire to alleviate some of the pressure that inherently comes with competing, as well as to expand her horizons rather than lock herself into a narrow path at such a young age.

"I wanted it to be like a highway, with all these different lanes available to me, and to go down all of them and see which one I wanted to focus on later on," she elaborated. "But I felt like I was on this little one-lane road, where it was all track and nothing else."

While she didn't pick up running again until her college years, Meredith certainly found ways to remain occupied: in high school, she played both basketball and volleyball for all four years. Although the teams were not extremely competitive, she enjoyed getting exercise in ways besides track. It wasn't until she started college as a non-athlete that she acknowledged the void running had left behind, since she had actively been involved in one sport or another for practically her whole life.

"Wow, this is the first time in ten years that I haven't been an athlete. And I didn't like that—I missed a sense of purpose because I didn't have anything else that replaced it," Meredith explained.

Used to living such a dynamic lifestyle, she felt uncomfortable not competing in any sport. It just so happened that Meredith knew that the girl living across the hall in her freshman dorm was on the cross-country team.

"I think I might've asked her, 'What are the coaches like? Are they nice?'" Meredith recalled. "I wanted to know if they would be open to hearing from me, having me walk down there, and explore the idea of running again.

"She was the one who actually got me to go, and then once I got down there, the coach was very open to having me join the team. He didn't commit to me being able to compete, but he said, 'I'll give you a tryout,' and then it just went from there."

When Meredith initially got back into running after a six-year break from the sport, her intention was not to become a professional athlete. But as she progressed and started conquering her more immediate goals, those avenues began to open up, as they came along.

"When I qualified for the Olympic Trials the first time, it was really kind of by surprise. I didn't even know what the standard was. It wasn't on my radar at all. I just was trying to do well at something else, and my coach said, 'Oh yeah, by the way, what you ran qualifies you for the Olympic trials.' It just kind of happened," Meredith recounted. "I just got to a certain milestone, and then at that milestone, I realized, 'Oh wait, now I can do this.' And then I'd go for that milestone, and then I'd say, 'Oh wait, okay, actually now that I'm here, it turns out I can do this.'"

Now, let me be clear. I am by no means suggesting that anyone can magically become an Olympic athlete by taking a six-year break from their sport of interest. But demonstrated by Meredith's success, taking a break is not always a bad thing. If nothing else, the intermission gives you enough time to catch your breath, put things in perspective, and decide whether the activity is something worth your time and worth pursuing. In today's society in particular, time is a highly coveted commodity.

* * *

BULLET JOURNALING

The latest modern trend is bullet journaling: the ultimate to-do list, which essentially integrates your journal, schedule, grocery list, notebook, and calendar into one little book, often tied together with some sort of artsy designs or doodles. Your latest and greatest business idea after binge-watching four straight hours of *Shark Tank*? Add it to the list. Keep forgetting to call your mom back after postponing for a couple of days? Throw it in the mix. Want to neatly organize a list of chores you have been avoiding? Why not. Chances are you've seen some Instagram pictures that capture the way someone magically transformed a boring to-do list into a work of art that makes you want to get things done.

In David Allen's book *Getting Things Done: The Art of Stress-Free Productivity,* he highlights that the biggest problem with most traditional to-do lists is that they are really incomplete lists consisting of "unclear things."[47] Based on Allen's philosophy, we should break down the content into three categories: next actions, projects, or reference material. However, one challenge that can arise with this classification system is that projects are pretty broadly defined, so this leaves room for other questions. What qualifies as a project? And what is the best way to break these so-called projects down into actionable steps?

When *New York Times* digital staff writer Concepción de León put this advice to the test, she found herself struggling

---

47   Allen, David. 2001. *Getting Things Done: The Art Of Stress-Free Productivity.* Penguin Books.

with tasks like meal prep, since it is a project that sneakily comprises multiple steps—finding an intriguing recipe, coming up with a grocery list, actually buying the ingredients, etc.[48]

I have always been a visual learner; I have a fondness for multicolored pens, notebooks, and school-supply shopping. I am one of those people who gets way too much joy from strolling through the aisles of Staples, throwing every type of organizational material into my basket, knowing that I will likely not even touch half of them.

Maybe it has something to do with the perceived benefits of these supplies, almost as if I will inevitably have my life "more together" if I have the physical tools to keep myself organized and on track.

I am a huge proponent of to-do lists, which typically include everything from "sauté zucchini tonight" to "buy shampoo" to "write history paper outline—seriously!!!" I find it inexplicably satisfying to write things down, to give myself the illusion that even if I don't have time to get everything on the list done that day (I never do), having a general awareness of what needs to get done puts me more at ease.

48   De León, Concepción. 2018. "The Art Of Bullet Journaling And The Improved To-Do List." *Nytimes.Com*. https://www.nytimes.com/2018/12/27/books/how-to-bullet-journal.html.

Freshman year, my roommate, Lily, and I would add the simplest things to our to-do lists, such as "take a shower"—primarily so we would reap the satisfaction of crossing that off the list even if we got nothing else accomplished that day.

But this method may not work for everyone. My boyfriend claims he has never owned a folder in his life. One time, I went to grab something from his backpack, and to my absolute horror, I found wads of crumpled-up papers settled at the bottom of the bag, crushed by the weight of his laptop and who knows what else. This man has *t-shirts* and *body wash* stored on the food section of his shelf in the pantry. That being said, I can't make fun of him too much, because this guy ran a multimillion-dollar business while he was a full-time student, published his own book before turning 21, and held an internship with the federal government while somehow still managing to get really good grades. As they say, there must be some sort of method to the madness—so who am I to judge?

The element of routine that accompanies writing things down can help eliminate stress. In high school, I prided myself on writing colorful, extensive study guides by hand before every European History exam. Each guide took me days to create, and my friends often made fun of me for it, but it worked out pretty well for me—despite leaving me with an incredibly sore right hand.

In the same vein, Doug Grant regularly keeps a gratitude journal. Additionally, he has come to value the power of meditation.

"I remember I got introduced to [meditation] in college years ago and then just put it down for forever. I never really thought about it again. But now there are so many apps for it, so it's so much easier. I just picked it up along the way and found a type that works for me. I think there's a lot of meditation techniques out there. But yeah, I think it's really, really important," Doug stressed.

Mitch Henkin has a million different tasks to complete each day, and he often needs to write things down in order to prioritize them. As a manager of a large number of employees, even in a relatively small business, he has a lot to keep track of and countless jobs to delegate.

Mitch always keeps a master calendar on the wall of the office, where his main administrative employees' names are listed, each in a distinct color. Next to the calendar lives a long blue chart with each employee's availability, organized under the location of that particular camp. After figuring all that out, he writes down the key dates in a compact, black journal and highlights certain ones to emphasize their importance. His system is quite distinct from the bullet-journaling method that compiles everything into one space. For Mitch, it's more about keeping track of everything in numerous places, locations, and colors to make sure it catches the attention of all his employees, as well as his own.

Because his personal iPhone doubles as his work phone, the only time Mitch gets a break from checking it is when he's swimming laps in the pool. Mitch used to run, but running aggravates his knees, so now he focuses more on other activities like swimming. So, despite the health problems he has encountered over the years, he finds ways to adjust his schedule to remain active and carve out that little chunk of time to focus on his well-being.

CHAPTER 7

STRONG SUPPORT SYSTEM

———

Rule No. 1: What happens in Vegas stays in Vegas. Or at least so I've heard. My family and I went on a trip to Las Vegas back when I was in middle school. It seemed like a bit of a strange place to take a wide-eyed twelve-year-old, but rest assured my parents did not allow me to gamble—I don't think I would've fooled anyone with my hot-pink bedazzled Vegas hat, as I proudly sported a shirt I had gotten at a friend's bar mitzvah weeks before and grinned from ear to ear.

In addition to the flashy hotels and the people decked out in elaborate costumes all along the Strip, I was entranced by all the optimistic hopefuls camped out at the casinos. I keenly observed their looks of determination and excitement and desperation and obsession.

Given my very limited knowledge of gambling, what I do know is that it inherently involves some sort of risky action, with the intent of achieving a desired result. And it can empty your pockets in a matter of mere minutes.

It was a total gamble for Jeff Iannaccone. Chances were slim.

You never want to fail a checkride. His examiner did something unique by giving Jeff the choice—ultimately the ball was in his court.

Jeff had his heart dead set on flying a fighter aircraft. Flying a big cargo airplane didn't interest him in the slightest. He had signed right on the dotted line, agreeing to owe ten years of service to the military after graduating from pilot training. Pilot training in the Air Force lasts a year, and the first six months in particular are extremely stressful, to say the least.

For the initial six months of training, everyone flies the same type of airplane; at the end of this period, everyone's scores on the graded rides are added together and you either become a fighter or a bomber pilot or go a different route and become a cargo pilot. Four of the graded rides are called checkrides, and these are the most pivotal since they effectively serve as exams.

"I put a lot of pressure on myself to make it through and be awarded a fighter. I'm stressed out, and when you're flying an airplane, you gotta be thinking with a clear mind—you can't be dwelling on the stress," Jeff explained.

The day before Jeff's first checkride, he choked.

"I just totally screwed up the ride. It was a horrible flight," Jeff remembered.

His examiner for that particular flight gave him an ultimatum of sorts once the ride ended. He turned to Jeff and said, "Dude, do you want to go to your checkride tomorrow, or do you want me to fail you on this ride and you can do it again?"

According to Jeff, you *never* want to fail a ride. When would a teacher ever candidly ask their own student if they wanted to pass or fail the test they were given? By doing just that, the examiner gave Jeff a rare opportunity to control his own destiny. It was all up to him now.

Jeff's checkride examiner calmly told him, "You've done everything you need to do up until this point; the preparation is there. You're freaking yourself out. You don't have to go be perfect out there. You just need to relax and go do the best that you can do, and you're gonna be fine."

That candor was enough to snap Jeff out of the bubble of pressure and stress that he had surrounded himself with.

I have prepared enough. I'm good, Jeff reassured himself, really believing it this time.

Ultimately, Jeff decided to take the first checkride the following day—and wound up finding great success.

"All I needed was one good one, one dose of success to get some motivation going—and I was on my way," Jeff recounted.

Jeff's story demonstrates that sometimes it can be easy to get caught up in the stress of a situation, especially in the workplace, and all that stress can make you lose sight of your fundamental goal and the preparation needed to get there. His flight examiner leveling with him and bluntly asking Jeff if he wanted to fail the ride gave Jeff the authority to voice what he really was after, and that proved critical for reminding him of his goal and reassuring him that he was capable and prepared and could indeed pass.

* * *

For Hannah Park, it was initially quite difficult to not be affected by her close friends' and classmates' troubles, which they would confide in her about. These were people she spent a lot of time with and in whom she was emotionally invested. Naturally, Hannah really cared about them, and it was taxing for her to see them struggle.

"It definitely impacts you when someone you care about is having a difficult time. But I think there were a lot of good resources for me to reach out to and ask for advice for my friends as well," Hannah acknowledged.

Given the high-pressure environment, Hannah applauded the strong support system that Juilliard offers to counterbalance the strain created by the institution's caliber of artists and its lofty expectations of them. Despite the tensions and stress that come with such an institution and its ambitious students, Hannah always felt like she could reach out to someone at Juilliard for help solving whatever problem was on her mind.

"I always felt like I had a faculty member or someone at school who had a similar experience who I could reach out to when I felt like someone was struggling too much," Hannah explained. "I didn't have to do a ton of searching if I was looking for a good counselor for them or anything. It was relatively easy for them to call health services and go straight away."

At Juilliard in particular, the small class size creates an intimate setting that allows for more personal attention and the fostering of close relationships compared to larger college campuses. Hannah effectively spent all of her time with the same select group of people from day one. Hannah recalled a number of incidents involving students grappling with serious mental health issues, but Juilliard tried to do everything in its power to be there for its students by offering free counseling services and psychiatry sessions, which helped a lot of Hannah's friends.

"For me, finding that one faculty member that I felt really comfortable talking to and who would sit and talk to me and try to make me feel better—that played a big part in me feeling happier at school," Hannah described. "I had a couple of close friends and my family and one or two faculty members who I could trust and talk to, and they were enough to calm me down whenever I felt things were out of control."

There is a neurological basis underlying the need for a strong support system. Humans are social animals, and forming relationships and connecting with others serves as the underpinning of our society. Emotionally arousing content can enhance people's sense of bondedness to a group. Based on the Dunbar study, strangers who watch an emotionally arousing film together are actually changed physiologically, as the material triggers an endorphin response and increases a sense of social bonding among viewers.[49] The same outcome does not occur when viewers watch films that lack emotional content.

Even if you don't wish to confide in anyone or don't feel ready to, what is most important is that you feel there is someone you *could* confide in. Just knowing there are people out there whom you trust—and who support and care about you and what you are going through—goes a long way.

Approximately one-fifth of college students today attend university at least 500 miles away from where they grew up. The astounding number of mental illness cases that emerge during the college years is in part attributable to the underpreparedness in American culture.[50] In the United States, there is a high prominence of cultural attitudes that emphasize the American desire for independence. But we have an autonomy dilemma of sorts: U.S. parents value autonomy and continue to reinforce fairly early departures

49 Dunbar, R.I.M. 2016. "Emotional Arousal When Watching Drama Increases Pain Threshold and Social Bonding." *Pubmed Central.* doi:10.1098/rsos.160288.

50 Rutherford, Markella. 2009. "Children'S Autonomy And Responsibility: An Analysis Of Childrearing Advice." *Research Gate.* https://www.researchgate.net/publication/225400720_Children's_Autonomy_and_Responsibility_An_Analysis_of_Childrearing_Advice.

from home—Americans leave the nest as early as offspring in other countries, such as Germany, Finland, and France.

However, in many other parts of the world, children shift away from dependence on their parents at a younger age. In Finland, for example, by the first or second grade, children typically have minimal supervision by teachers and parents, and young children are permitted to stay out after dark. Japanese children brush their own hair, dress themselves, run errands, and take the subway to school on their own by the age of six or seven.[51] In contrast, children in the United States today are less likely to be without supervision than in previous generations or than their peers in other countries. The American cultural value of autonomy encourages students to attend university far from home, but the transition is abrupt due to the absence of societal practices to help prepare students for this newfound independence.

In 2018, over 60% of college students said they had experienced "overwhelming anxiety" in the past year, and over 40% reported feeling so depressed that they "had difficulty functioning," according to the *New York Times.*[52]

51 Hoy, Selena. 2015. "Why Japanese Kids Can Walk to School Alone." *The Atlantic.* https://www.theatlantic.com/technology/archive/2015/10/why-japanese-kids-can-walk-to-school-alone/408475/.

52 Wolverton, Brad. 2019. "As Students Struggle With Stress and Depression, Colleges Act as Counselors." *Nytimes.Com.* https://www.nytimes.com/2019/02/21/education/learning/mental-health-counseling-on-campus.html.

Even though many universities have recently expanded their efforts to offer students professional counseling services, the demand has exceeded the services provided.

"We would love to provide all the resources to all the students," said Christopher Brownson, associate vice president for student affairs and director of the counseling and mental health center at the University of Texas at Austin. "But the answer to all social and emotional problems in the world cannot be to go see your therapist."[53]

Although counseling resources should be provided for those who need them, there are other useful initiatives that universities can undertake to promote their students' mental wellness.

The University of South Florida in Tampa found that about a quarter of their students who sought counseling didn't need a therapist but could benefit from assistance with developing their coping skills. To help students address their anxiety and improve their time-management skills, the university created "relaxation stations" with massage chairs, bean bags, and nap pods, which instantly became the most "sought-after seats on campus" the *Times* reported.[54]

---

53   Ibid.
54   Ibid.

It undeniably took me a while to open up and get to the point where I was comfortable enough to share how I was doing with others in a way that didn't feel like I was burdening them. But once I finally got there, it proved invaluable. It can take a while to open up to people, and that's okay. There is a happy medium between keeping everything pent-up and broadcasting your whole life story to the world through a megaphone. It is about finding that middle ground where you feel most comfortable. You can always choose to confide in certain people on particular topics and others on distinct areas of your life—it is strictly a matter of personal preference.

CHAPTER 8

FOCUSING ON THE LITTLE THINGS

"It's like family: you don't have to love them, but you love them anyways."

Hannah Park compared the distinct schedules of an average college student and a student at Juilliard, concluding, "I feel like I talked to all of my friends who went to 'normal' schools, and it's definitely a very different experience. My brother's schedule is much more flexible."

At Juilliard, you do not get to choose any of your classes; the minute you enroll, your schedule is practically set for you. From 9–10:15 a.m. every day, the first- and second-year students all have an academic period. During their third and fourth years in the program, they have some sort of guest-related subject. In Hannah's case, she had anatomy, and there were guest speakers who came in and shared their experiences with the class.

From 10:40–12:05 Hannah's class had ballet, then modern dance from 12:15–1:40, which was followed by lunch. After lunch, repertory class was held from 2:30–3:45, where they learned works that had already been created. From 4–8 p.m. each day, the students had rehearsals for performances that the school sponsors; there are three main ones every year: new dances, spring repertory, and the choreographing honors.

After that, the window between 8 p.m. and midnight was the only block of time students had to rehearse with any student groups they were part of. Because of the rigorous schedule, it is nearly impossible to find time for any outside activities or excursions, let alone time for yourself.

"The Juilliard faculty really wants to develop their students as artists, so they have these things that are workshops, performances entirely made up of student choreographed works," Hannah explained. "Anyone from any year can be asked to be in one.

"I was in quite a few student-choreographed things. They take up a significant amount of time, but sometimes it's more interesting than things you do in school."

These student-run pieces range between three and eight minutes in length and are performed for the rest of the school and faculty members every three months. These workshops present Juilliard students with a unique occasion, since it is difficult to get that kind of experience after graduating because of the high costs and challenge of finding people to work the studio for you, so students tend to take advantage of them, adding yet another layer onto their already hectic schedules.

When asked how she manages her health and whether she is able to find a balance given her chaotic routine, Hannah replied that moving off campus made a significant difference for her.

"I think at first it was hard, like first and second year especially," Hannah admitted. "I lived in the dorms, and the dorms and the school are connected by this walkway, so you don't even have to touch the street level to get to school. There's this thing called the 'Juilliard Bubble,' when you can go weeks at a time without touching the sidewalk, without experiencing the city. You get caught in that. It was really difficult at first."

"It felt like I was always at school and never really got to step away. You literally spend 9 a.m. to 9 p.m. with these people for four years. First and second year, you spend twenty-four hours a day, seven days a week with the same people. We're all really close friends now, but at first it was really competitive."

Hannah's class initially started out with twenty-four students total, and twenty ended up graduating together.

For many college students, moving off campus with a group of friends is a highly anticipated and coveted transition, and students can hardly wait to escape their cramped dorm rooms and the scrutiny of their RAs. For Hannah, this wasn't the case; she thoroughly enjoyed the solitude and freedom of living alone.

"Being away from the Juilliard buildings and going somewhere I considered home was a big relief for me. It made going to school and being around the same people a lot easier. It made a big difference for me," Hannah elaborated. "I am the kind of person who needs a second to myself every once in a while. Just being able to come home and be alone for a second and read or listen to music helped relieve a lot of the stress from being at school."

Finding little ways to promote your wellness can be extremely beneficial in the long run. For Hannah, it was living alone off campus that made the difference, by allowing her a little extra time to herself, which was crucial for her to nurture her health, given the high stress environment during her college years.

* * *

Others find solace in having a routine. For Doug Grant, it's all about establishing a morning ritual and taking time to meditate. While pursuing his MBA at Georgetown, Doug took a class that focused on the importance of having a balance between work and life outside the workplace.

"I like getting the most done in the morning. Waking up early—that's my ideal state. And I don't do this every day, but I feel like I have what my wife calls my ritual. I aim to get up around 5:30 a.m. I've already made the coffee the night before. When I get up, I have two glasses of water, a cup of coffee. I do like some stretching, a little yoga," Doug described.

Part of Doug's morning routine involves meditation. He used to use an app called Headspace, but he now uses the app Calm to help guide him through his relaxed state. After meditating, Doug typically engages in a little bit of prayer and does some journaling before kicking off his day.

"So when I'm on that routine, that's when I'm at my best. I think like physically, spiritually, mentally. If I can do the ritual, I know I'm on track," Doug explained. "I did this morning, and I'm having a great day so far. That's something I've been doing just these last couple of years that I think has really been useful. I wasn't doing that during Hemeos, the startup, and I wasn't doing that during the Navy. But I'm a big believer in meditation now. I'm really, really into it."

Likewise, Mitch Henkin values his morning routine. Although not as structured as Doug's, Mitch aims to simply eat breakfast while reading a hard copy of the newspaper each morning before diving into the craziness of running a small business. For Mitch, it's all about making an effort to carve little spaces for personal time throughout the day, no matter how hectic.

* * *

THE POWER OF HUMOR

"Well, I think it has to do with being mindful that balance is necessary. And I know as a team leader that you can push your group just so far before they need a rest and they need to see the humorous side of things. So I try to inject humor."

When asked about effective leadership, Steve Worth, now an international management consultant, immediately launched into a story from his days attending a boarding school in the 1960s. He recounted in detail one time at school when there was an enormous amount of stress among his fellow students, as the majority of assignments seemed to be due at the same time. Steve points out that these were very intelligent students, but they saw themselves going down in flames, so to speak, because of all these simultaneous impending deadlines they had to meet.

The headmaster called a general assembly, and the students were all wondering, *What is he going to say? Is he going to chew us out?*

Unsure of what was to follow, all the boarding school students gathered, only to find their teachers dressed up in comical costumes, making fools of themselves up on the stage.

"Laughter was just uproarious and everyone was just . . . we had to release that energy somehow and see the light side of things. And he knew how to do that," Steve recalled.

The headmaster himself was known as quite an extraordinary person; he graduated with an Ivy League degree and served as a bomber pilot in Europe during the second World War. His plane was shot down over Holland, and he was taken prisoner by the Nazis, but he orchestrated an escape and was later rescued by the Dutch underground. Overall, he was an extremely intelligent guy with an eventful past—a natural leader, as evidenced by the vast respect his students had for him.

"He was a legitimate hero," Steve declared. "You could see he was a man who was very much in control. But he was the one who orchestrated this foolishness just to let it all out, let the tensions out. So I think there are tricks like that leaders use. . . . It requires them to know where their team is, and you need to help them along in certain times."

In addition to the power of humor, Steve illuminated the idea that granting people breaks at certain critical times is a key component of effective leadership, and that compelling leaders seem to know when it is necessary.

"A good team leader knows how to get the best of the team by coaching them along and allowing the tensions to work themselves out, or giving people time off that need it," Steve added.

Jeff Iannaccone similarly noted the influence and sway of humor in his leadership technique, even in settings that are typically perceived as utterly serious—in his case, the military.

"I think taking a Patton-esque approach to it, even in the military, is completely wrong," Jeff emphasized. "I practice servant leadership—to lead by example, as opposed to taking other routes to get there. And I like to think of myself as an easygoing person, and that has always served me well. I feel like it brings about the better in people because you're able to take pressure situations or stressful situations and kind of dilute that for your team members, and they are able to accomplish a heck of a lot more by doing that."

Humor isn't solely useful in eliciting a chuckle; it actually has significant power. Studies show that feigning a smile can eventually create that reality. Babies start smiling around eight weeks old through the process of imitation and positive reinforcement. Children have certain inherent biological tendencies they bring into the world. If a baby is smiling, they will evoke smiles from those around them, which over time can help create a more socially responsive person.[55]

On top of the importance and sway of humor, Jeff stated that the first thing that he does when he is trying to motivate a team is ensure he is being true to himself.

---

55 Scarr, Sandra, and Kathleen McCartney. 1983. "How People Make Their Own Environments: A Theory Of Genotype → Environment Effects." *Child Development*. doi:10.2307/1129703.

"I could talk about leadership for hours," Jeff confessed. "I love the topic, but it is so complex. I really do feel that way. I need to be true to myself and know my own personality and know how I am comfortable interacting with people, and I am not going to fake it."

One predominant thread in Jeff's encounters is the impact of being genuine. It may sound simplistic, but being genuine when he stands up as a leader and tries to motivate everyone to accomplish the given mission at hand has gotten him far.

"I am very honest with myself and I don't try to put on some disguise. I think leadership and mental health play together from that standpoint," Jeff pointed out.

While resources such as therapy and counseling are invaluable in promoting wellness, other informal mechanisms, such as humor and honesty, can be quite impactful as well. Humor can go a long way to nurture health and relieve stress, as demonstrated by Steve's impeccable memory of his high school headmaster's command of leadership and the value Jeff places on being genuine and true to himself. There is something very human and universal about humor in particular, and it has a way of uniting people, both inside and outside the workplace. The role of humor in the workplace is especially pertinent when it comes to being mindful of how to effectively manage a team and working with others in somewhat stressful scenarios.

* * *

AVOIDING ANGER

Apart from humor, avoiding anger when possible can also be an effective strategy to enhance communication and promote overall well-being. Doug Grant finds it helpful to momentarily back away from a situation that incites anger or extreme stress.

"I think I've gotten better as I've gotten older at not making immediate decisions emotionally," Doug explained. "If you just step away from something, don't hit send on the email, you know—realize what your mental state is, and that it's not going to really help you in that moment. Just getting up and walking away from something is probably sort of my default now, as opposed to when I was younger—I might have been more in the moment with a 'let's just do this' attitude. I think that it's good just to pause and stop."

Additionally, Doug has found that when in stressful or awkward situations that require balancing personal relationships with business ties, it is best to have some sort of agreed-upon accountability metrics to help address the problems and ease the tensions.

"It's about separating the person who you care about from the action and behavior. I think if you can separate things, it makes having those difficult conversations a little bit less stressful," Doug remarked. "I'm not going to say 'a lot less stressful' because I'm by default very conflict-avoidant. And that's something I've learned about myself. And you have to learn your own behavior and what makes you tick and what gives you anxiety. I'm not a confrontational person, so it's easier for me to avoid those hard conversations."

Back when Doug was in the Navy, he was confronted by some people with vulgar, contemptible personalities. The reality is that there are people like that in every setting, so it's best to find ways to put aside your differences and collaborate with them, or at least try to get along.

When recounting his experiences with these kinds of personalities, Doug recalled, "If you don't acknowledge that or talk with me and confront that head on, in some ways, you're going to internalize it, and then you're just going to be angry at that person or angry at yourself for not confronting that person about it. That's the worst, right? Because you were trying to be conflict-avoidant, and then all you did was internalize it, and it made you more anxious, more angry, more frustrated."

Anger has the power to subconsciously cause someone to make choices that will only fuel their angry state. For example, when people read a story about an injustice that evokes anger, they exhibit stronger interest in reading further about injustice.[56]

While feeling anger is a natural human process and inevitable emotion, evidence suggests angry speech can be detrimental to your overall well-being. Speech can be considered a form of violence if the words cause prolonged stress, which could in turn lead to physical harm.[57] Even when no physical contact is involved, words alone can kill neurons and actually shorten your lifespan. Although there are good kinds of stress, such as that evoked when trying to take someone else's perspective that you don't agree with, psychology professor Lisa Feldman Barrett suggests that we must halt speech that bullies and torments: hateful speech.

56 Green, Jeffrey. 2017. "Self-Enhancement, Righteous Anger, And Moral Grandiosity." *Self And Identity.* doi:10.1080/15298868.2017.1 419504.

57 Feldman Barrett, Lisa. 2017. "Opinion | When Is Speech Violence?" *Nytimes.Com.* https://www.nytimes.com/2017/07/14/opinion/sunday/ when-is-speech-violence.html.

Doug reflected on instances when he successfully kept his strong emotions in check, as well as when he failed to do so. He had to engage in a tough conversation with his fellow startup co-founder, but found that going back to their established accountability metrics was quite helpful.

"'You know we said we were going to do this by this day, and we haven't.' So I was like, 'I love you and care about you and you're my friend, but what's going on? This isn't going to get us to where we need to be.' So that was a good way of handling it," Doug recalled.

On the other hand, when Doug was in the Navy, he attempted to deal with a more senior lieutenant, whom he found pretty irritating. His frustration with the lieutenant and his leadership style prevented Doug from standing up for himself and confronting their differences head on. Instead, Doug internalized his resentment toward the lieutenant and became frustrated with himself. In retrospect, he recognized that having an honest, candid conversation with the lieutenant to express his anger would have been more productive.

"Telling him that 'this is unacceptable to me from a point of respect'—that would've been a much different conversation. And that would have been much healthier at that point in my life," Doug admitted. "But that didn't happen. So I think that's recognizing that I know I'm conflict-avoidant, but at one point in my life I did something better with that knowledge. The other time I didn't do something as well with it. So it's kind of like learning as you grow older."

Doug pointed out that often just trying to be more self-aware and recognizing your own triggers and anxiety points can be helpful moving forward. It's critical to be honest with yourself and recognize what your own weaknesses are before you are able to really start doing something to overcome those faults.

* * *

Although I've striven for perfection for the majority of my life, over the years I've learned how to take it easy. Paradoxically, I had to put in a noticeable amount of effort to get myself to relax.

In a sense, my hitting an all-time low was what it took for me to examine my lifestyle in a new light and reevaluate my choices. Not having enough time for myself and feeling like I constantly had to be running around busy all the time played a significant role in my successive breakdown. It took me hitting a wall and crashing and burning before I realized how important this time is for both my own mental and physical health.

Up until recently, I struggled to give myself breaks because I always felt like there weren't enough hours in the day to get everything done, and I felt guilty if I took a moment to rest or stop to catch my breath. I had a hard time fully relaxing because I always felt like I had some homework or essays or chores or some other responsibilities hanging over my shoulder. But I quickly learned that kind of mindset is a sure way to send you into a tailspin.

I have begun to carve out more "me" time into my hectic schedule, whether that's binge-watching *The Office* in my bed, going to the library with friends rather than alone, or as simple as treating myself to a midday nap when I've had a tough day. Finding time for yourself isn't always easy, and sometimes it involves sacrifices or having to step back and re-prioritize things to fit it in. Whatever your method is, this is super important to do—I can't stress that enough.

If you find yourself experiencing something like I did or worse—a panic attack, anxiety, depression, feeling over-whelmed, suicidal thoughts—*please* tell someone. Tell anyone: a friend, family member, teacher, or counselor, and make that first step toward getting help. You are absolutely not alone and don't have to go through it on your own. You will find a lot of support out there. I can promise you that.

As evidenced by all these raw and honest stories, there are a variety of techniques that work to improve mental wellness for different people. My aim was to shed light on some of the seemingly simple, nontraditional, informal mechanisms that promote mental wellness and overall well-being. I aspire to play a role in raising awareness of mental health issues and combating the associated stigma. I hope you will join me in the effort and the ongoing journey for achieving mental well-being.

ACKNOWLEDGEMENTS

———

First and foremost, I'd like to thank my family. Mom, thank you for the innumerable hours you spent tirelessly editing my manuscript after I couldn't bear to look at it any longer. Dad and Ben (if you're reading this), thank you for supporting me and providing comedic relief along the way. Thank you to all of my amazing friends and family for the countless laughs and for lifting me up whenever I am struggling. Also, thanks for putting up with my occasional heated rants and dramatic storytelling.

Thank you to all my interviewees—it was fascinating to hear your stories, and I appreciate you taking time out of your busy schedules to speak with me about such an important topic.

A special thank you to everyone who pre-ordered my book. Your generous financial support made its publication possible, and words can't express how grateful I am for this opportunity. I want to take a moment to individually thank everyone who contributed:

Elsa Friedman
Marcos Morales
Debra A. Felix
The Friedman Family
Toni Koh
Debra and Steve Cardon
Beth Pincus
Letitia Carlson
The Block Family
Karen Dubrow
Lily F Zino
Jaime Yepez
Evan Roberts
Amanda Pirri
Lauren Seibel
William Zacek
Hannah Everett
Haley Callicott
Heidi Pilpel
Heidi Dupler
James Koh

Paul and Jo-Ellen Kosack

Eric Koester

Gabriella Jeffords

Abigail Fry

Robert and Kerry Levin

Chris Sebastian

Melissa Urofsky

Michele McNally

Kenneth Ramsey

Rick Alfonso

Susan Hendrickson

Susan Callicott

The Morales Family

Gigi Jones

David S Koh

Julia Heller

Emily Ma

Nadia Finkel

Shivani Goyal

Nicole Lam

Ben Friedman

Julie Billingsley

The Cowles Family

Rachel Moss

Jonathan Isaacs

Cira Mancuso

I couldn't have done it without all of you, and your support means the world to me!

Last but not least, a huge thank you to the New Degree Press team—especially Eric Koester and Brian Bies for making this all a reality.

APPENDIX

INTRODUCTION

Davey, Graham. 2013. "Mental Health & Stigma." *Psychology Today.* https://www.psychologytoday.com/us/blog/why-we-worry/201308/mental-health-stigma.

Friedman, Michael. 2014. "The Stigma of Mental Illness Is Making Us Sicker." *Psychology Today.* https://www.psychologytoday.com/us/blog/brick-brick/201405/the-stigma-mental-illness-is-making-us-sicker.

Love, Kevin. 2018. "Everyone Is Going Through Something | By Kevin Love." *The Players' Tribune.* https://www.theplayerstribune.com/en-us/articles/kevin-love-everyone-is-going-through-something.

U.S. Department of Health & Human Services. 2019. "What Is Mental Health?" MentalHealth.gov.

CHAPTER 1

Davey, Graham. 2013. "Mental Health & Stigma." *Psychology Today*. https://www.psychologytoday.com/us/blog/why-we-worry/201308/mental-health-stigma.

Kwai, Isabella. 2016. "Today's College Students Are Not Less Resilient." *The Atlantic*. https://www.theatlantic.com/education/archive/2016/10/the-most-popular-office-on-campus/504701/.

"Mental Health By The Numbers | NAMI: National Alliance on Mental Illness." 2018. *Nami.Org*. https://www.nami.org/Learn-More/Mental-Health-By-the-Numbers.

"Oberlin College | Office of Equity Concerns | Support Resources for Faculty." 2019. *Oberlin Office of Equity Concerns.*

http://web.archive.org/web/20131222174936/http:/new.oberlin.edu/office/equity-concerns/sexual-offense-re-source-guide/prevention-support-education/support-re-sources-for-faculty.dot.

Pressly, Linda. 2017. "Sweden's Mystery Illness." *BBC News.* https://www.bbc.com/news/magazine-41748485.

Swanson, JW. 2015. "Mental Illness and Reduction of Gun Violence and Suicide: Bringing Epidemiologic Research to Policy." *Pubmed Central.* doi:10.1016/j.annepidem.2014.03.004.

CHAPTER 2

Blackburn, Paul. 2018. "Brené Brown on the Power of Vulnerability | Global Success Academy." *Global Success Academy.* https://theglobalsuccessacademy.com/brene-brown-ted-talk/.

Connors, Joanna. 2018. "How a Transplanted Face Transformed Katie Stubblefield's Life." *National Geographic.* https://www.nationalgeographic.com/magazine/2018/09/face-transplant-katie-stubblefield-story-identity-surgery-science/.

McCandless Farmer, Brit. 2018. "John Green's Advice: Don't Forget to Be Awesome." *CBS News.* https://www.cbsnews.com/news/john-green-advice-dont-forget-to-be-awesome-60-minutes/.

CHAPTER 3

Beresin, Eugene. 2017. "The College Mental Health Crisis: Focus on Overall Wellbeing." *Psychology Today*. https://www.psychologytoday.com/us/blog/inside-out-outside-in/201703/the-college-mental-health-crisis-focus-overall-wellbeing.

Francis, Perry, and Aaron Horn. 2016. *Campus-Based Practices for Promoting Student Success: Counseling Services*. Ebook. https://www.mhec.org/sites/default/files/resources/20160215SS7_counseling_services.pdf.

Gottfried, Sydney. 2017. "Is 'Sleep When You're Dead' Georgetown University's Unofficial Motto?" *HuffPost*. https://www.huffingtonpost.com/sydney-jean-gottfried/is-sleep-when-youre-dead-_b_8917488.html.

Kwai, Isabella. 2016. "Today's College Students Are Not Less Resilient." *The Atlantic*. https://www.theatlantic.com/education/archive/2016/10/the-most-popular-office-on-campus/504701/.

Rasch, Björn, and Jan Born. 2013. "About Sleep's Role in Memory." *Pubmed Central*. doi:10.1152/physrev.00032.2012.

Simon, Caroline. 2017. "More and More Students Need Mental Health Services. But Colleges Struggle to Keep Up." *USA Today*.

https://www.usatoday.com/story/college/2017/05/04/more-and-more-students-need-mental-health-services-but-colleges-struggle-to-keep-up/37431099/.

"Starting the Conversation | NAMI: National Alliance on Mental Illness." 2019. *NAMI*. https://www.nami.org/About-NAMI/Publications-Reports/Guides/Starting-the-Conversation.

CHAPTER 4

Barnard, Brennan. 2019. "Six Terms to Stop Using in College Admissions." *Forbes*. https://www.forbes.com/sites/brennanbarnard/2019/01/11/six-terms-to-stop-using-in-college-admission/#3af6d3391aed.

Gray, Peter. 2015. "Declining Student Resilience: A Serious Problem for Colleges." *Psychology Today*. https://www.psychologytoday.com/us/blog/freedom-learn/201509/declining-student-resilience-serious-problem-colleges.

Iyengar, Sheena, and Mark Lepper. 2000. "When Choice Is Demotivating: Can One Desire Too Much of a Good

Thing?" *Journal of Personality and Social Psychology*. https://faculty.washington.edu/jdb/345/345%20Articles/ Iyengar%20%26%20Lepper%20(2000).pdf.

Kwai, Isabella. 2016. "Today's College Students Are Not Less Resilient." *The Atlantic*. https://www.theatlantic.com/ education/archive/2016/10/the-most-popular-office-on-campus/504701/.

Soodik, Nicholas. 2017. "High School Students Are Applying to Too Many Colleges (Essay) | Inside Higher Ed." *Inside Higher Ed*. https://www.insidehighered.com/admissions/ views/2017/12/04/high-school-students-are-applying-too-many-colleges-essay.

Strauss, Valerie. 2016. "Why Harvard 'Encourages' Students to Take a Gap Year. Just Like Malia Obama Is Doing." *The Washington Post*. https://www.washingtonpost.com/news/ answer-sheet/wp/2016/05/01/why-harvard-encourages-students-to-take-a-gap-year-just-like-malia-obama-is-doing/?utm_term=.7ef03825a39d.

Thorne, Gabriela. 2018. "Mental-Health Care on College Campuses Is Broken—This Group Aims to Change That." *The Nation*. https://www.thenation.com/article/mental-health-care-on-college-campuses-is-broken-this-group-aims-to-change-that/.

CHAPTER 5

Davey, Graham. 2013. "Mental Health & Stigma." *Psychology Today*. https://www.psychologytoday.com/us/blog/why-we-worry/201308/mental-health-stigma.

Publishing, Harvard. 2009. "What Causes Depression? - Harvard Health." *Harvard Health*. https://www.health.harvard.edu/mind-and-mood/what-causes-depression.

Wallace, Jean. 2017. "Mental Health and Stigma in the Medical Profession." *Sage Journals*. doi:10.1177/1363459310371080.

CHAPTER 6

Allen, David. 2001. *Getting Things Done: The Art Of Stress-Free Productivity*. Penguin Books.

De León, Concepción. 2018. "The Art of Bullet Journaling and the Improved To-Do List." *The New York Times*. https://www.nytimes.com/2018/12/27/books/how-to-bullet-journal.html.

CHAPTER 7

Dunbar, R.I.M. 2016. "Emotional Arousal When Watching Drama Increases Pain Threshold and Social Bonding." *Pubmed Central*. doi:10.1098/rsos.160288.

Hoy, Selena. 2015. "Why Japanese Kids Can Walk to School Alone." *The Atlantic.* https://www.theatlantic.com/technology/archive/2015/10/why-japanese-kids-can-walk-to-school-alone/408475/.

Rutherford, Markella. 2009. "Children'S Autonomy and Responsibility: An Analysis of Childrearing Advice." *Research Gate.*

https://www.researchgate.net/publication/225400720_Children's_Autonomy_and_Responsibility_An_Analysis_of_Childrearing_Advice.

Wolverton, Brad. 2019. "As Students Struggle With Stress and Depression, Colleges Act as Counselors." *The New York Times.*

https://www.nytimes.com/2019/02/21/education/learning/mental-health-counseling-on-campus.html.

CHAPTER 8

Feldman Barrett, Lisa. 2017. "Opinion | When Is Speech Violence?." *The New York Times.* https://www.nytimes.com/2017/07/14/opinion/sunday/when-is-speech-violence.html.

Green, Jeffrey. 2017. "Self-Enhancement, Righteous Anger, and Moral Grandiosity." *Self And Identity*. doi:10.1080/15 298868.2017.1419504.

Scarr, Sandra, and Kathleen McCartney. 1983. "How People Make Their Own Environments: A Theory of Genotype → Environment Effects." *Child Development*. doi:10.2307/1129703.

www.ingramcontent.com/pod-product-compliance
Lightning Source LLC
Chambersburg PA
CBHW071523180526
45171CB00002B/358